A Question of Spirit

Andrew Macpherson

WGA Manuscript Registration #

ISBN: 9780988502222

Target—Adult
ISBN: 0988502224
Library of Congress Control Number: 2014917589
Macfly Corporation, Los Angeles, CA

TABLE OF CONTENTS

THIS BOOK IS DEDICATED TO MY FATHER.
IT WASN'T UNTIL HE PASSED THAT
I REALIZED HOW MUCH HE'D LOVED ME,
HOW MUCH HE'D HAD MY BACK,
AND HOW MUCH HE'S STILL HERE FOR ME.

Introduction

What if reality, as many mystics have suggested, really is just an illusion? The intricate matrix of the subatomic is so different from our reality that those who study it describe it as being akin to another dimension. Matter, the foundation of our universe, is a holographic dance of energy. Its particles aren't solid things, they're electromagnetic charges constantly pulsing together, defining matter's mass with their frequency.

So what if life is nothing more, or less, than Spirit's way of communing with matter? Could looking at the interplay of Spirit and reality lead us to a deeper understanding of all that is, and give us a new way to experience reality and each other? Those are the questions that inspired this book. By embarking on this journey of discovery, you'll see the beginnings of a way to move beyond the constrictions of religion and find a new understanding of all that is, in this dimension and the next.

So what is Spirit? If we are all Spirit bound to matter in this journey of life, where does it come from? Where does it go? Does it exist beyond time? How is it addressed in different religious teachings? What is its place in the modern world of science? We're inundated by TV shows about psychics, mediums and ghostly hauntings, but these never get to the heart of the matter. There is plenty of evidence that when Spirit leaves the body it lives on, but where, how and as what?

In my twenties I had a series of personal experiences that bridged the veil between the what-is and the what-is-not. I started dreaming of things that in the following days happened exactly as I'd seen them. Some seemed irrelevant, like snippets of a conversation overheard on the escalator in the subway, but others were stone-cold serious, like dreaming of a colleague having a miscarriage before she'd told anyone she was pregnant or seeing the twin towers come down six years before 9/11.

However, the impact of my dreams was eclipsed by my experiences with Spirit.

It started slowly at first, with little glimpses of things here and there, but it was enough to send me to spiritual bookshops in search of answers. I muddled through poor explanations in books that never rang true and talked to several 'psychics' who were either tricksters and fakes. We're all guilty of looking for answers in the wrong places, but in those times before the Internet, there wasn't anywhere else to turn. Spirit kept coming through clearly enough to make me certain it wasn't just a figment of my imagination. Unable to find any satisfactory explanations for my experiences, or anyone knowledgeable enough to discuss them with, I kept a journal of them.

Experience always trumps belief, but in the case of Spirit, it also creates far more questions than answers. My hunger to understand this drove me to do the research that resulted in this book, and I've laid out what I discovered in much the way it unfolded.

The first section is a compilation of stories from friends and colleagues that presents compelling evidence of Spirit through experience. When I started the book, I asked my then thousand-strong circle of acquaintances on Facebook if any of them had any experiences with Spirit to share. Almost one in ten had, or knew someone who had, so I started by interviewing almost a hundred people. I found that their perception of both the "here and now" and the "ever after" had been completely changed by their interaction with Spirit. I picked the ones I found the most compelling, recorded them, had them transcribed, and then checked for accuracy by the interviewees. I believe the stories in this section prove that there is no question of the existence of Spirit and its ability to influence our lives for the better.

For the second section, I interviewed a group of renowned mediums to get the perspective of those who work with Spirit day in and day out. Most of them have already been published, several have their own TV and radio shows, and they all came highly recommended. I also had a reading with each of them before doing their interviews, and they each proved to me that they were genuinely able to call in Spirit.

For the third section, I asked each of them the same set of questions to explore what we can understand from the other side. Their answers are not all the same, but at their core, they are harmonious in illustrating that there is far more to this dimension than either science or religion has an explanation for.

For the fourth section, I interviewed a group of scientists to get an understanding of what we know about the universe on the cosmic and subatomic scales. While they humbled me with their knowledge, they also pointed out that science is the study of what is, the measurable, and thus it has a natural resistance to Spirit, the immeasurable, the what-is-not. Their interviews were in such a harmony that I ended up editing out a couple of them to avoid repetition.

Since we can't test or measure Spirit in a lab, it remains truly mysterious, but science itself is becoming ever more mysterious. In 1925, we knew of just one galaxy, ours, but today the Hubble Space Telescope has shown us that there are at least a hundred billion galaxies in the visible universe and likely many times that amount beyond. Our instruments have imaged the cosmic microwave background, the inside of the expanding shell of the big bang. However we don't know what was here before the big bang or what our universe is expanding into. Dark matter was proven to exist eighty years ago, but we still can't measure it. We see dark energy at work in the accelerating expansion of the universe, yet we don't know what it is or where it came from. These two immeasurables are said to account for 96 percent of the weight of our universe, while everything we know, the stuff of you, me the planets and the stars, is just 4 percent. Even though we're living in the golden age of learning, we're constantly confronted with the limits of our knowledge. Science turns yesterday's mysteries into today's truths, but they in turn will be swept aside by tomorrow's discoveries, reminding us change is the only real truth.

For the fifth section of the book, I interviewed three spiritual leaders to get their perspective on Spirit, karma, and destiny. I chose them from outside the warring tribes of Abraham because the faith of my Christian birth never spoke to me. As a child, the endless wars, inquisitions, holocausts, and genocides over which is the right way to believe made a mockery of the Ten Commandments. The Old Testament is the core of the world's three main religions, yet in several passages it preaches against mediums and Spirit: *A man or a woman who is a medium or a necromancer shall surely be put to death. They shall be stoned with stones; their blood shall be upon them* (Leviticus 20:27). I don't see this as a great way to treat someone with an extraordinary gift or gain a greater understanding of the true nature of Spirit. It reads more like the dictate of a cult terrified of anything beyond its control. The endless wars and inquisitions over the righteous interpretation of ancient tales of long-dead kings, carpenters, and shepherds always seemed tragically misguided to me, and for what? A book, written by people who believed the world was flat, with none of the wisdom or learning we have available to us today. I believe we need a new understanding of Spirit, a story that unites the world, not divides it. Creation's greatest gift is the unfolding of present, the here and now.

The devoted and loving worship of the deities of the past has given us spectacular monuments. We marvel the pyramids of Egypt and South America, Stonehenge, the Acropolis, Angkor Wat, Mecca and the Vatican, the world is covered with beautiful temples built in praise of the gods and goddesses. They illustrate the extraordinary power of man's need to believe in a higher power, however they don't prove any of those gods or goddesses actually existed.

Today, the gulf between science and religion dwarfs the Grand Canyon, and their differences are constantly debated with passion, animosity, and anger. To the men of knowledge, religion looks like a triumph of ignorance, an emotional attachment to the superstitions of the past. To the believers, all this knowledge just challenges their faith, belief, and certainty. Both are looking into the void of the unknown in search of answers, but both are confined by their dogmas and their struggle for dominance.

Without addressing the breadth of the unknown with humility and love, there is no hope of either party broadening its horizons. However, between these two dueling perspectives are those of us who through direct experience know there is something incredibly mysterious beyond the scope of either science or religion, and that is Spirit.

I wrote this book to help me understand Spirit, but the more I dove into it, the more I found there was a loftier goal I'd love it to realize. If we as a civilization could open a new (and civil) conversation about Spirit and reality beyond the confines of religion, or the constriction of science, we might have a hope of finding an idea of Spirit that unites us, rather than divides us.

Never before have we been closer to a global culture, and never before have we so needed a universal understanding that recognizes we are of the universe. That's uni as in one, one creation, one love, one force, one source. I believe the only way we can reach that understanding is through and with Spirit.

Section One

The Experiences

Chapter 1

JOHN BROMLEY

The first time I heard John Bromley's name was in June 1988. I was working as a young fashion photographer at the time and had just flown to Los Angeles from London with Naomi Campbell to do a shoot for *Harpers & Queen* magazine.

Back at the hotel after a long day's work, Mary, our makeup artist, invited an old friend of hers, Doe, to join us for a drink. As Doe strode into our chalet at the Sunset Marquis, I was immediately struck by her delicately exotic beauty. A Navajo woman in her thirties, she was graceful and charmingly polite, yet preoccupied and somehow cloaked with an overwhelming aura of sadness. When she left, Mary explained that her husband, John Bromley, was suffering from an extreme case of manic depression, or bipolar disorder as it's called today. It started slowly at first, but throughout the last decade it had taken over his life, sweeping him away in its violent mood swings for weeks at a time. His erratic and often scary behavior had alienated the clientele at his successful restaurant on Sunset, driving the business to ruin and destroying their marriage. I knew nothing of his condition or its implications, but Doe's story snapped into focus the tragedy of a life torn apart by something beyond the reach of medicine.

Two months later I was in Miami on another fashion shoot when Mary phoned me from her room distraught. Doe had just called to say that John had taken his life the night before. He'd finally given up hope of finding any way out of the depression that was destroying his life and the lives of everyone he loved. It was a dark finale to a heartbreaking tale, but, sitting in my hotel room in Miami, it wasn't something I imagined would change my life.

Four months later I was headed back to Los Angeles for another shoot. As the almost empty TWA 747 made its final turn to LAX, the city's main airport, I was glued to the window. Banking in over the San Gabriel Mountains that separate Los Angeles from the desert, I was lost in view of the city stretching away to the sparkling ocean eighty miles to the west when a voice right behind me said, "You're coming home."

I spun around, but there was nobody there. I jumped up and scanned all the seats around me, but there wasn't anyone within five or six rows. After a long moment staring into the almost empty plane searching for a reasonable explanation of what I just heard, I was forced to accept that there simply wasn't one, so I sat back down and considered the words. There was no way I could be "coming home." My home was in London, and as a fashion photographer all my work was between there, Paris, and New York, so I put it out of my mind and gazed back out the window again.

My oldest friend from school, Simon, had moved to LA a year or two earlier and fallen in love with California's majestic landscapes, so I arranged to stay on for a few days after the shoot to do a desert tour with him. Not only would I get to spend some quality time with my oldest friend, but I'd also find some new locations and get to soak up some sun before heading back to London's winter chill.

The evening before our adventure, Simon suggested we eat dinner at a restaurant he loves. I picked him up in my rental and drove us down Sunset Boulevard to a plain-looking little building opposite the imposing Chateau Marmont. Stepping inside, we entered another world. Sultry, smoky, and sexy, it was a dash of Marrakech mixed with an English gentleman's club, shaken, not stirred. As the glamorous female Maitre d'î sashayed toward us through the crowded room, I realized it was Mary's friend, Doe. I offered her my condolences as she showed us to our table, and she thanked me graciously as she sat us. After dinner, when the busy pace of the restaurant quieted, she joined us for a coffee. Sitting down, she flipped her hair, trying to crack a smile, but it didn't hide the sadness in her eyes. I asked how it was going. She took a long breath, stared into our empty coffee cups awkwardly, then lifted her head slowly and told us that losing the man she loved and taking over his restaurant has been the hardest thing she's ever done. She was yearning to escape, to get away and forget everything.

I mentioned we were heading out to the desert in a rented convertible with a trunk full of supplies inspired by Hunter S. Thompson and his legends of being wild in the West. Without missing a beat, she asked if she could come, too. After hearing everything she'd just been through, there was no question. "Sure, we'll pick you up at nine," I said.

On our way to collect Doe the next morning, Simon and I agreed that a woman in mourning must be left respectfully alone. However, after a wonderful drive through the mountains, an afternoon of laughter, and dinner at the 29 Palms Inn with too many margaritas, it was clear she was craving love, tenderness, and to be appreciated for the beautiful woman she was. A little drunk, dazed and confused, I navigated between the voice in my head saying it was wrong and the compassion in my heart cheering for love. On the way back to our cabins, Doe and I somehow found ourselves locked in a passionate embrace under the desert stars. During the next few days, we fell deeply into each other in the most beautiful, natural, and honest way.

Sunday evening, our desert adventure behind us, we drove back into the city's sparkling lights. I dropped Simon off at his place in the canyon beneath the Hollywood sign, then turned and headed for Doe's. That's when it really hit me, I was going to be taking her back to John's apartment.

Over the weekend I'd learned a lot about him and the hole his departure had left in her life. Born in England about twelve years before me, John had a background uncannily similar to my own. We were both from the same layer of a very layered society, went to similar schools, frequented the same bars and clubs in London, and we both felt trapped by the confines of England's rigid class structure.

Carrying Doe's bags up from the underground parking lot, I got my first glimpse of John's world. High, vaulted ceilings and large, comfortable couches echoed the restaurant's sultry, bohemian feel. Stepping inside their home, the weekend's stories of him came rushing back. I felt like I shouldn't have been there so I started to say good night, but Doe asked me not to leave. The idea of spending the night in his home with his wife made me very uneasy, but I also knew I couldn't refuse her. My apprehension grew climbing the stairs, but his world stopped when she opened the bedroom door. This was clearly Doe's domain. Even though it had the same bohemian feel of the main room, it was set apart by a delicate feminine sensuality. Dark velvets, plush pillows, and a deep down duvet all beckoned my weary bones.

Our night together passed peacefully, and we both slept soundly until the alarm went off at dawn. Doe got up and went to the restaurant for an early delivery, leaving me alone in the apartment. I walked her to the door, then went to the kitchen to make some coffee. As the kettle boiled the hairs stood up on the back of my neck and a chill ran through me. He was there, I could feel it. I looked around but couldn't see anything, so I just started talking to him: "John, I mean no harm to Doe or disrespect to you. I am very sorry for the situation that forced you to take your life, but I just want to make her happy and help her move on."

Breaking the ice felt good, so I kept talking, telling him how much I liked the apartment. Looking through his books and his incredible record collection, I pulled out some of the unique discs and discussed them as if he were beside me. By the time Doe returned, I was completely at ease with both John and being in the apartment.

Over the next fourteen months I constantly felt him there but never saw or heard anything that was proof positive. During that time Doe's biological clock made having a baby her most pressing issue. I loved her, but being several years her junior, I knew it wasn't my time to be a dad, so to use her words, "Shit, or get off the pot."

Breaking up sucks, especially when you both adore each other.

It was late January when I left the apartment for the last time. It felt so terribly final watching Doe wave me good-bye bathed in the street lamps' orange glow as I climbed into my ride to the airport. Back in London, I kept tabs on her through our mutual friends. I heard she'd met an amazing man, married him, and was pregnant, but rumor also had it that the pregnancy had been fraught with difficulties.

It was Christmas Eve in 1992, and I was home with Maria, a girl I'd just started seeing. My house was also my studio, office, and darkroom so it was always buzzing with the comings and goings of work, but the holidays brought peace and quiet. We turned the house into a cozy love nest and let the world outside fall away. As the empty city hibernated, we shared stories of the things we'd done, places we'd been, and the rides we'd taken on life's merry-go-round. Telling the story of my time in LA, I pulled out a box of photos to show her how beautiful it is and found a collection of vintage film-studio publicity prints that John had bought from an old movie memorabilia store. It was a wonderful potpourri of Hollywood's golden age in silver gelatin: Marilyn, Dietrich, Keaton, W. C. Fields, Bogart, and Valentino, all printed on the kind of beautiful photographic paper that they haven't made for years. Doe and I brought them back to my darkroom to turn them from gray-looking publicity printouts into richly toned master prints, but they ended up getting forgotten in a print box in the darkroom. I started telling Maria about John, but was immediately interrupted by a voice right inside my head, as if I were wearing headphones. It wasn't any thought of mine; it was clearly someone speaking to me. It said, "Call Doe and tell her that everything is going to be all right with the pregnancy."

"Maria, did you hear that?" I asked.

"No, hear what?" she replied.

"I heard a voice," I replied. My thoughts went straight to Doe. I knew that this was her last chance to have the child she wanted so badly. The last thing I wanted to do was pick up the phone to give her a message from a voice in my head!

It came again, though this time more forcefully: "Call Doe now and tell her that everything's going to be all right with the pregnancy."

"Surely you heard that?" I asked, but she just shook her head.

Then the voice shouted its demand a third time, so loudly that I almost jumped out of my skin. "You must have heard it that time?"

"No." she replied.

I told her what I'd just heard, but her reply really caught me off guard. "My mom's Romani, she hears spirits all the time. You'd better do as it asked and call her."

Palms sweating, I picked up the phone. How do I tell Doe a voice in my head told me to call her, especially after not talking to her for a couple of years? What if this message lit a flame of false hope? It would just amplify the pain of things going wrong. Swallowing hard, I put my doubts aside and did as I'd been told. I dialed and waited, hoping for a machine. Doe answered. I told her the whole story from the beginning, the box of prints, talking about John and his life, and the voice suddenly coming, quietly at first, then so insistently. I told her I wasn't going crazy, and I prayed she didn't mind me calling. At first, she was silent, then I heard her quietly weeping, and my heart sank. I'd broken an unbreakable rule. Then she softly whispered, "Thank you, John. Andrew, let's talk later. Thank you, too."

The rest of the pregnancy passed trouble free, and three months later she gave birth to a healthy and strong baby boy. All John needed was to give Doe his blessing and his assurance, nothing more, nothing less. In talking about him, giving him the focus of my attention, I built the bridge just enough so that he was able to cross it and deliver his message. He reached out to me in hope that I'd give him a voice in that moment, and I accepted the responsibility of being his messenger.

Five years later, I'd left London's dull gray skies behind for good and was splitting my time between New York and Los Angeles, the city I was told would be my home was really opening its doors to me. However, finding a home of my own took another nine months, a dozen realtors, and almost two hundred house visits. Finally, a realtor told me I was looking in the wrong area. I protested it was where I wanted to live, but she was adamant, it was time to look elsewhere. On our second trip I found myself standing in the garden of a house looking right down at John's old apartment. He liked things dark and closed in, but I'm a lover of light and views. Every time I had walked out of his old place, I'd looked up at the houses on the hill above Sunset basking in the bright sun and said to Doe, "One day I want to live up there."

Standing in the garden, I felt his presence once again. Maybe it was just because I was thinking about him, but this house had been on the market for ten months. The seller, an actor who won her Oscar when she was living there, had had two sales collapse at the very last moment, and now, right before Christmas, was very motivated to sell. Today, almost twenty years later, I'm writing this story looking out at that same 180-degree panoramic view of LA, and the street where John's old apartment was.

After moving in, I constantly felt his presence when things happened like the stereo turning itself on and off, CDs changing randomly on their own, lights turning on and off and even catching little sparkles of bright blue light in the corner of my eye. Doing all the interviews for this book has taught me that playing with electronics, especially TVs, computers, and stereo systems, is completely normal spirit behavior.

A couple of years after moving in, a friend who shares my fascination with the mysteries of life called with word of a psychic of great repute who was visiting from London. I phoned him, and a few days later we were sitting on my balcony, his tarot cards spread on the table before me as he divined the future in the summer-afternoon sun. Gazing into the cards, he told me I was going to photograph spirits, and that it would be with my work equipment, the cameras I used every day. I would think there was something wrong with them, but there wouldn't be. It would be the spirits.

A few months later, my friend Claudia Navone, then a fashion editor at *Elle* in London, came to LA to do a pair of stories with me for the early summer issues. As usual, she stayed in my spare room, and the rest of the crew stayed at the recently opened Standard Hotel just down the road. The first story was shot at my house with Carolyn Park, a model Claudia had worked with before. Claudia also was interested in all things psychic and told me Carolyn had the gift. Of course I was intrigued by this and couldn't wait to meet her, and the team, for an early breakfast. We said our hellos, ordered our coffees, and started to chat. Carolyn talked in a broad Yorkshire accent and had a five-pointed Wiccan star tattooed on her wrist. When I asked her about it, she sidestepped the question, instead telling me she hadn't been able to sleep because the hotel was full of spirits that had kept her awake all night. She asked if I knew what the hotel was before its recent refurbishment, and I told her it had been an old folks' home. In her thick accent, she replied, "Of course, that's why so many people have passed over here."

After breakfast we did her hair and makeup in her haunted hotel room then headed up the hill to my place. As Carolyn walked in my front door, she looked at me with grave concern and said, "Ohhh, there's spirits in here, I can feel it!"

"Don't worry, it's just John. He's a friend," I reassured her. Much to my amazement, she started talking to him as if he were right there in the room with us. Of course to her, he was. As we started shooting, she carried on her conversation with him, discussing all kinds of things, mostly humorous and trivial. I kept a mental note of all that was said during the two days so I could check it with Doe to be sure it really was John.

This experience took place just before Christmas in 1998, in the days before digital when we'd set up our shots using Polaroid film in our large-format cameras. I'd been using the same Mamiya RZ67 camera and

Polaroid film holder for about fifteen years so of course knew exactly what to expect from it.

As we started shooting, little flecks of light inexplicably appeared in the Polaroids, streaking across the normally black, unexposed areas out of frame and all the way onto the image. I tried sealing out any stray light that may have been causing it with black camera tape, but the streaks got stronger. My assistant, Alex, was convinced I was playing some sort of trick and asked me how I was doing it, but I assured him it wasn't me. Then I showed the photos to Claudia and Carolyn and told them what that psychic said about photographing spirits. They smiled at each other in that way girls do when they're both in on a secret.

I clipped the film back onto the camera and started shooting. Within a few frames Carolyn's attention to the camera evaporated as she launched into an unseen argument with John about the music. Apparently he hated what she was listening to and told her he wanted Tchaikovsky. "No way! I'm working, so I get to choose!" she snapped back.

A fast-paced ping-pong match of wits flared up between them as I tried to keep her focus on shooting our fashion story. They talked of music, hats, suits, and cars, with Carolyn filling us in on his part of the conversation. It was the first time I'd been witness to a conversation with a spirit as if he were in the room with us, but now I understand how such a powerful connection can bring a spirit back into our dimension, and allow its energy to be captured on film.

On the second day of the shoot, both John and the streaks of light were even more apparent, but by that point we were all used to Carolyn's invisible conversation. She and John riffed off each other for hours as we worked through the remaining outfits. As the last roll of film wound itself out, I clipped the Polaroid film back onto the camera and took a final frame to check that everything had worked properly. I pulled the sheet of Polaroid film out of the camera and put in under my arm, which is something all us photographers used to do to speed the process. It took around ninety-seconds for a Polaroid to develop properly, so in that time we all headed back upstairs for lunch. Casually, I peeled the Polaroid open, and my jaw dropped. In all my years using it I'd never seen anything like this, nor do I have an explanation for it.

Here is that image, made on the same Polaroid 669 film and Mamiya RZ67 camera that I worked with both as an assistant and a photographer from 1975 to 2005, and during this shoot was the only time I saw this happen. The black border is the unexposed part of the film outside of the camera's 3.25-inch by 3.25-inch (7-centimeter by 7-centimeter) imaging area. Type 669 film came in a sealed light-tight pouch that you'd tear open before putting it into the Polaroid film back. Even if you left it sitting around out of the pouch, the cartridge is still completely light tight. Once inside the Polaroid back, the cartridge is completely sealed with no way for light to get in and streak across the unexposed (black) area of the image.

So what of Tchaikovsky, and all the other things thrown around in their invisible conversation? I checked the details of everything with Doe. John played Tchaikovsky in his restaurant every December because he thought it the perfect music for Christmas. Our shoot was in early December. John loved hats, classic cars, and always wore a suit. Not only was he irreverent, playful, and wickedly funny in life, but also in spirit, he carried all that over with him.

It was my experience with John that gave me the insight and inspiration to collect the stories and ideas shared in this book. John continues to play with the stereo and the electronics in my house to this day, much to my, and Apple help desk's annoyance. Of course now I'm certain it was he who told me I was 'coming home' on that TWA flight all these years ago. I also credit him with making this house my home and feel his invisible hand in many of the wonderful things that have happened here in Los Angeles, the City of Angels we both love and are proud to call home.

Chapter 2

Carolyn Park

More than a dozen years later, I tracked Carolyn Park down again, and she gave me the following interview over the phone.

AM: *Carolyn, I've done thousands of shoots in my thirty years as a photographer, and ours was certainly the most unique. What do you remember of it?*

Carolyn: I remember feeling a presence as soon as I came into your house, then seeing this guy in my mind's eye. He showed me various things he liked, like the classic cars. He had a very strong frequency vibration, and I saw those beautiful lights that we caught on the film everywhere. It was like a dance, dancing with an entity. His energy was really easy, fun, and somehow familiar, like meeting an old friend I'd known for years. Him being there made the two days very fun, special, and unforgettable.

AM: *How did your interaction with Spirit begin?*

Carolyn: When I was three or four, my mom got divorced, and we moved into an old farmhouse down a big, winding track a mile and a half from the road. I started getting terrible night terrors there and would sleepwalk through the house. During them I'd be back in medieval England, even though I was in a dream it felt so real, it was just like being awake. It'd always start in my bedroom, which was full of people I didn't know running around, so I'd leave to get away from them. Sometimes my mom would walk into the dream, and I'd ask her to wake me up, but she couldn't. She said my eyes were always open and full of terror, and it looked like I was trying to run away from something. She even found me walking around the bottom of the farm track a couple of times. I remember always seeing this woman called Annie, with a baby in her arms, screaming for me to help her. Awake, I didn't know her, but in the dream I was really aware of who she was, and I knew I had to help her. I'd even shout out to my mom that we had to help her.

My mom said I'd also talk a lot about being in London at the time of the fire and the plague in 1666. I'd go on and on about that period as if I was living in a past life. My mom took me to a child psychologist who said it was all just emotional and was only happening because I was missing my father. Honestly, I think that was a load of shit, he had no idea what he was talking about. I believe we can tune into these memories from the past, whether they are our past lives or other lives that have been lived. Either way, I'm sure that it was my conscious mind just trying to deal with these unresolved issues from the past by reliving them.

AM: *Were either of your parents psychic?*

Carolyn: My mother's extremely sensitive, very emotional, and an excellent judge of character, but she wouldn't say she's psychic. Honestly, I think she closed herself off to it, but for sure it comes from her mother and that side of the family.

AM: *What was your next major experience with Spirit?*

Carolyn: A few years later, when I turned eleven, my mom fell in love with a cottage in a tiny village called Snape in Yorkshire, and we moved there. Just at the end of the high street was a huge, thousand-year-old castle. It's still lived in, so it's quite well preserved. I was immediately smitten with the place, it touched something deep inside me and I'd spend every day going up there. I'd even skip school just to go.

One afternoon while I was in the chapel, I picked up a leaflet about its history and started reading it. My eyes get stuck on this name, Richard III, then a powerful energy brushed by me. I spun around and caught a clear image of him in my mind's eye.

The next time I saw him was in the cottage. At first I felt his powerful presence, then I saw him again in my mind's eye. He talked with a great deal of kindness and respect, but he was angry that he wasn't remembered as the great and good king he was. He said the Tudors paid Lord Stanley to betray and murder him and have his name besmirched with their propaganda. He told me that Elizabeth I employed Shakespeare to write the play *Richard III* to make him look like a monster, and the terrible story of the two young princes being murdered in the Tower of London had nothing to do with him. That was all arranged by the church.

He was never frightening or threatening to me, and I could tell by his energy that he was a kind and gentle man. He asked me to write down everything he said. Back then my mom had an early computer, so I'd write it all down as he asked, and after a few months I had enough to make a book. Then something happened to the computer and everything on the hard drive got wiped out.

AM: *Were you convinced he was innocent of history's charges?*

Carolyn: I ask myself that all the time. How do you ever know if someone is lying, whether it's a spirit or person? He was always respectful to me, but he had an intense temper. When I had people in my life who were bad for me, especially boyfriends who denounced my gift, he'd get extremely angry. His energy was so strong that I'd be afraid he'd do something bad to them, but looking back, I honestly feel like he was a sort of guardian angel.

A few years later, I came across the Richard III Society and discovered much of what he'd told me had since been proven, like the fact that he never had a hunchback. It was added to the painting of him a hundred years later.

AM: *Did you ever contact them to give them your story?*

Carolyn: No, because honestly I didn't want to be ridiculed, but I did call them to say that I loved what they were doing. You really can't communicate with too many people about this sort of stuff, there's just too much fear about it.

AM: *If you've already opened that connection, would you consider starting that book again? I know it's something I'd love to read.*

Carolyn: No, not really. That was all a long time ago.

AM: *That makes sense, but I'd still love to hear more of what he'd have to say. Thanks so much for sharing your story with us.*

* * *

Since this interview, Richard III's body has been discovered in the City of Leicester. The publicity has once again brought forward the question of his reputation, which has been reexamined in light of all the new historical information. It's now accepted that Shakespeare was writing for the pleasure of a popular audience. Their monarch, and his, was the extremely popular Elizabeth I, so any story that glorified the Tudors and made the vanquished king look like a monster would have been very popular with both the crowd and the queen.

Chapter 3

Claudia Navone

I first met Claudia Navone in the late eighties when she was working as a junior fashion editor at *Elle* magazine in London. Coming from an old Italian family whose ancestry included two popes and several other historically important dignitaries, she always brought exceptional class and style to her work. We bonded through our shared passion for fashion and our interest in the mysterious, often talking late into the night about the nature of destiny, karma and Spirit. A few years after I moved to LA, she left *Elle* and London, immigrating to Sydney to become the fashion director at *Harpers Bazaar* there. As so often happens with friends in very different time zones, we drifted apart, so when I rang her in Sydney to get her remembrances of our shoot with Carolyn, I was totally surprised to discover Spirit had changed her life, too.

AM: *When did your experience with Spirit begin?*

Claudia: In the early nineties, when I was living in London and working at *Elle*. One summer afternoon I was relaxing with some friends in their garden when the conversation drifted to our friend Nadia, who'd died of HIV a couple years earlier. Suddenly I felt myself slipping into a sort of trance. My eyes were still open, but everything went dark like someone turned down the lights. Then I started talking, but it wasn't me, it was Nadia speaking through me. Even though I knew it was her I didn't really hear what she said as she gave everyone messages and answered their questions. It just sort of flowed through me and when I came out of the trance I didn't remember any of it, but everyone was buzzing about what she'd said.

It wasn't long after that I got the offer to be chief fashion editor at *Bazaar* in Australia. I'd always wanted to live in Sydney so I jumped at the chance, but little did I realize what Australia had in store for me!

A friend lent me his apartment in Tamarama, and as a welcome gift gave me two beautiful tortoise totems made by a known Aboriginal artist. They were quite mesmerizing, and I'd often look at them before bed. One night as I was gazing at them a light spiraled up out of one of them, and morphed into a fine, radiant blue vision of the tortoise. I rubbed my eyes trying to make sense of it as it started flying around me. This went on for a good couple of minutes, then the blue light just zipped back into the tortoise. I knew I'd seen something both real and extraordinary, so I immediately Googled the totem, the artist, and his tribe. It turned out that their creation legend was based around life coming from the stars in the shell of a tortoise.

From that moment I was drawn to their culture, and immersed myself in its art, stories, dreams, and legends. Of course that inspired me to do a fashion shoot at Ayers Rock, in the center of Australia, so I went there with a full fashion crew. It was every bit as beautiful and magical as I'd expected. Our shoot went really well, and we managed to get everything finished early so we could have a day off to enjoy the place. After breakfast we went out to a series of rock formations called the Olgas that I'd read were very spiritually powerful, and are just a little way off from Ayres Rock, but offer a beautiful view back at it.

Walking through the giant boulders, I got separated from the others, and started feeling a bit disoriented. Suddenly a voice as powerful as thunder shot right through me. "Stop! Go and sit on that rock and wait there in silence for twenty minutes, then the only male in your group will come and get you."

Scared, confused, and wondering if I was going mad, I did as I was instructed. Then I heard it again: "He's coming to find you now. After you rejoin the others I'll give you some messages and show you a sign so you'll know this is real."

I waited patiently on the rock until, as the voice predicted, the only guy on our team came to take me back to the others. My photographer was also very much 'of spirit', so I knew I could confide in her. I told her what just happened and she suggested we stay behind to see if the voice would return. We tell the others we'll see them back at the hotel, and set off on our own over the rugged red terrain.

It's usually pretty crowded at the Olgas, but there was nobody around as we made our way through the beautiful rock formations. Finding a good vantage point, we sat to look out at Ayers Rock and absorb the beauty and the stillness of the place. Suddenly the voice returned, putting me straight into some kind of trance. I started singing in a language I didn't know, then channeling things about my friend's life. After that the voice said, "Now you can go, but before the end of your walk, Spirit will reveal itself to you."

I came out of the trance, and into an uneasy normality. My friend took my hand, and with a smile said we should go. We stood up and made our way back towards the car, but half way there a white kangaroo burst out from behind the red rocks. We both froze as it bounded towards us in enormous leaps. It was on us in an instant, and my first thought was that it's going to attack us, but it stopped a couple of feet in front of us, looked us in the eye, turned, took one bound away and vanished into thin air! We both looked at each other in total disbelief, did that really just happen?

That was moment I realized a part of me was completely unexplored, and I wanted to stay there to discover it, but my deadlines in Sydney wouldn't allow that.

Back in the frantic flow of work and the fanfare of fashion, I experimented with drugs to see if they'd get me back in touch with that force. They did open the gates of my perception, but not in a good way. I saw bad things, dark beings, like little gremlins attached to people. One night at some supposedly fabulous party, a group of demonic hissing fairies appeared in the bathroom mirror. Another night I was in a nightclub full of people I didn't know who are all really excited to meet this powerful being who was about to appear. I became convinced it was the devil who coming, and bolted out of there as fast as I could.

A few days after that I found myself in a house full of demons shouting my name, telling me that if I followed the dark path I could have anything I wanted. Every cell in my body screamed *RUN!* Desperate to escape the darkness I dive into a hole in the wall and frantically clamber through it praying they wouldn't grab my legs and drag me back in. Outside the sky is crystal blue, the fields are vibrant green, and the sun warm and welcoming on my skin. From nowhere a voice told me I had a very special gift, but that I had to choose between the dark and the light because both wanted me. Sobbing, I blurted out that I wanted to be in the light.

"Good, we welcome you into the light, but you must never again take drugs."

I swore I wouldn't, and I haven't since that day, nor will I ever again. The next morning I called my mother, who's both psychic and very spiritual, to tell her what happened. She told me to put a glass of salted water by my bed each night for a week, or until the water is clear in the morning. The first day it was dark and murky when I woke up, but with each day it got clearer and clearer, letting me know I'd cleared too.

After that everything settled back into an easy equilibrium for a few weeks, until one morning, sitting at a cafe by the office with a cappuccino, something incredible came over me. A voice right inside my head said, "Do not be afraid. I'm an angel, and I have a message for you. In a few days you'll meet a teacher who'll help you begin your spiritual transformation. Trust your instincts and follow the path."

A little shell-shocked, I headed back up to the office and sat at my desk again wondering if I was going mad. Within a minute an old friend called to say she's going to spend the weekend with a spiritual teacher called Qala in Byron Bay and asked if I wanted to come, too. Of course I said yes!

The workshop was amazing, and during those two days I awoke to Spirit in a whole new way. It was the beginning an extraordinary six years of study with Qala, who'd go on to teach me to see everything as interwoven dimensions of energy, and connect to the healing wisdom of the Ascended Masters.

After that first weekend I knew my life had to change, but fashion was my first love, my passion, and I wasn't ready to turn my back on it. Fate intervened just a few short weeks later when the editor of our magazine, who I adored, was fired. The new regime made me realize I loved working for her, not the title, so I resigned.

The freedom of my newfound freelance life gave me time to pursue my spiritual studies, so I booked a trip to Egypt with Qala for three weeks. Being there unlocked something deep inside me, and during my meditation the Ascended Masters instructed me to let go of everything and surrender to Spirit. I was told to leave my work and success behind and commit to a life of service. It was a deeply profound experience and set me on the path I'm now walking.

After returning from Egypt, I was guided to Berlin to work with John of God. He is one of the most powerful healers in the world and the embodiment of light, love, and service. I recognized the healing entities he channels, and that confirmed my decision to live the rest of my life in service, using what gifts I may have for the greater good.

My first night back home in Sydney, sitting in meditation, a pillar of light enveloped me. My guides came through again telling me to give up everything; my possessions, my clothes, and my profession. I'm to keep no more than two suitcases of things so I can travel freely, and I must return to Europe because my work is needed there. It takes me by surprise, but I surrender to the divinity.

Getting rid of everything was made really easy for me. Within a few hours one friend bought all my furniture and the fashion gang snapped up all my clothes. I left for Europe with no plan except to trust, and follow my calling. Of course I was nervous because in fashion my life was scheduled to the minute, and now I had no plan and no idea how people would react to my calling, but the trip was amazing. Everyone was incredibly open and I found many people who needed my help. I discovered the deep gratification of witnessing people turn their lives around and come into a place of happiness, health, and harmony through our work together. I really fell in love with being in service, and channeling the healing energy of the Ascended Masters.

AM: *So who and what are the Ascended Masters?*

Claudia: You could call them angels and archangels because that's the kind of energy they possess. They are literally light and love, yet they exist in a different dimension. The ancient holy men knew how to connect to them, which is why their archetypes turn up as religious figures in so many ancient scriptures around the world, but they aren't connected to any religion.

AM: *So what about God, does God exist?*

Claudia: Yes, of course, but not in the biblical sense. God is the Source, God is everything. We are all a part of God, and inseparable from God.

AM: *How has experiencing that affected your work?*

Claudia: I've progressed to the level of the Keepership of the Rays of Creation, which means I'm now able to access my own spiritual superconsciousness, the divine presence we all have at our cores. Through it the wisdom, love, and healing energy of the Ascended Masters are always available, which helps me channel their healing energy quickly and effectively. I don't do the work, they do the work, I'm just the conduit, but I'm getting to be more of a broadband connection now.

AM: *What do you do with this connection to the Masters?*

Claudia: I help people align with their greatest potential, empowering them to manifest the life they truly desire. Some just want to be cancer free, others want to get over addiction or make a project happen. Some want to find their own spirituality or shift their consciousness, and some are just searching. It doesn't matter why someone comes to me because each light worker holds a piece of the puzzle, and those in need are always drawn to the right one.

Doing the work I stay within my own column of light, and those I'm working on are in their own column of light. So I don't have to be in the room for the work to happen, but the person I'm working on has to really want to make the change in his or her life. Change happens on the inside, and from my perspective, it starts with peeling away the negatives, fear or loathing, and bringing in love. So many people are sick or living in sadness and insecurity because they don't love themselves. They think they're never pretty enough, rich enough, or successful enough, or go through life comparing themselves to others. Getting to the heart of that, and letting that darkness go, allows the light of love to shine, and once they learn to love themselves, the change they desire is unstoppable.

I feel so blessed knowing that this work is my true purpose here on earth and to be following such a powerful higher calling. I'm living life fearless and absolutely free, letting my guides tell me where to go and what to do. It really is divine, a word we'd use a lot in fashion, but with no idea of what it really means.

AM: *What a great story, and congratulations on having the courage to follow your calling, and making such an extraordinary personal transformation.*

Chapter 4

CAMPBELL MCAULEY

Campbell McAuley is one of the world's great hair stylists. His work has graced the covers of many magazines, including *Vogue*, *Glamour*, *Cosmopolitan*, and *Allure* as well as advertising campaigns for Victoria's Secret and Guess. We've worked together on many projects over the years and in many ways have been witness to each other's spiritual journey.

AM: *How did your experience with Spirit begin?*

Campbell: When I was seven, we moved into an old house in Killara, a suburb of Sydney. It was built in the mid-eighteenth century as the main manor of the old orange orchards that filled the area before it was developed in the thirties. We bought it from the family of the second owners, yet the only person living there was the old matriarch, and once the sale was complete, her family moved her to a nearby retirement home. About a year later, my brother Matthew and I were playing in the front room when she burst in wearing a yellow bathrobe, yelling at the top of her voice, "Get out of my house! Who are you, and what are you doing here? Get out now!"

Matthew and I were terrified, and hearing the commotion, mom came running and tried to calm the old lady down. Eventually, she came to her senses, mom sat her down in the kitchen, made her a cup of tea, and called the retirement home to come and pick her up. A couple of days later, we heard she passed away and realized she just wanted to come home to die.

About a week after that was when I first glimpsed the milky silhouette of a woman in my bedroom doorway. I mentioned it to Matthew and my mom, and over the next few days they both saw and sensed her around the house. Then one evening while I was getting into bed, she walked right up to me, bent down, kissed me on the cheek, turned and walked away. That's when I really knew I could see spirits.

The next time something like that happened was when my brother turned sixteen. He'd started studying Druid and pagan religions, and decided to do a seance at the house. He asked our cousin and a friend over to see if we could contact the old lady, then we set up a room with candles and the Ouija board. When they arrived we turned out the lights, lit a candle and sat down to ask our questions. Sure enough, the glass started moving around the board, but being kids we each thought it was the other mucking about, so we all agreed to take our hands off the glass. We counted to three and lift off it at once, but the glass kept moving, spelling out her name. Then she told us what she liked and disliked about each of us, which totally freaked us out. We put our hands back on the glass to stop it, but the power pulling it around was too strong.

My cousin said, "I don't believe this, this is bullshit. If this is really true, make the candle wick go up high." Immediately the flame leapt over a foot in the air and he bolted out of the room! Matthew and I quickly thanked the old lady for coming through, apologized for disturbing her, and closed the session.

AM: *Tell us a bit more about Matthew.*

Campbell: Matthew was four years my senior and an awesome older brother. He always was an old spirit, even though he was young, and somehow we both knew he wasn't going to live a full life. Looking back, I realize I never saw him being fifty.

When he was seventeen, he moved to San Francisco and became a dancer, which disconnected us for almost a decade. Those ten years were very important to both our development in different ways. I stayed in Sydney being a teenager, partying and figuring out what I wanted to do, while Matthew was dancing with Tina Turner. Once I really got into working with hair, I moved to London, and lived there for five years perfecting my skills. During that time I'd visit Matthew in LA or Vegas on the way back to Australia for the holidays and got to see him dance in some of the big shows on the Strip. He was such an amazing dancer, he was always so spectacular on stage.

AM: *When did he become ill?*

Campbell: Just after I moved back to Sydney to start my own salon was when he was diagnosed. He was very straightforward about having HIV and didn't really care where or how he got it. He was adamant about not coming back to Sydney, and my mother couldn't leave home to take care of him. That triggered something inside of me, I just knew I had to go to LA to be with him. It wasn't an easy decision because I was already getting entrenched with a salon, staff, and doing all the hair for Australian Fashion Week, but once I made the decision, everything just started opening up. I met my agent, and she asked if I'd thought of going to LA. I told her my story, and within a few weeks I was on a plane, paid for by a client, on my way to spend the last years of Matthew's life with him. Knowing our brotherly and spiritual connection was going to be broken was really daunting, and coming to LA to rekindle our relationship was the best decision I've ever made.

AM: *Did you talk about him connecting to you in Spirit once he passed over?*

Campbell: Yes, we had wonderful conversations about his life, how he wanted to be remembered, and what he'd like us to do with his remains. He had a total acceptance of his circumstance and of the unknown, with a strong belief that his spirit would be free in many different dimensions. When people see spirits they think they're in our time and our reality, but what we see and know here in life is just a minuscule slice of an endless amount of possibilities and realities. Matthew wanted to live but wasn't afraid of dying, and he knew that death wasn't the end, but a rebirth. It's very profound remembering the things he said when he was alive and only realizing the full extent of those conversations now that he's gone.

AM: *What happened when he passed?*

Campbell: We went for our weekly Chinese dinner, and he was being his usual big-brother self. He made me promise to call him if ever I decided to marry the girl I was with, but he wouldn't say why. He talked about his career and being a dancer at thirty-three. He felt he couldn't dance like he used to and was worried he looked like a dad amongst all the younger dancers. Then he said he didn't think he had much time left. He'd just finished his drugs and was riding out a bout of sickness hoping it wouldn't turn into anything more serious. I could feel he was really worried this time, and driving him back home, I told him not to get down, that I was there for him and I wouldn't let him go. The next day my mother called out of the blue. "Campbell, there's something wrong with Matthew, I can feel it. You have to go there now, please!"

I was already on set and we weren't going to be finishing till late, but I promised her I'd go first thing tomorrow. She called before my alarm went off, frantic, scared and upset. I calmed her down and said I'd go over right now. I drove straight to his place, let myself in, and called out to him, but there was no reply. I walked up to his bedroom to make sure he wasn't asleep, but his room was empty. Then the guy he shared the house with came in and said he was out with him last night, and he was fine then. I immediately thought that's so my brother, out somewhere having fun with friends while everyone's worried sick. I called my mom to let her know everything's fine, he was just out with friends.

The next morning she called again, crying. "Something's wrong with Matthew, really wrong. I can feel it. Something terrible has happened."

I was already at work on a TV commercial, and I knew I'd be on set till midnight, so I calmed her down, promising I'd go around first thing tomorrow. That night I got a text saying I had to be on another set super early. I called Matthew but it went straight to voice mail, so I left a message telling him to call Mom because she's worried sick, and I'd be over after work.

That morning driving to the studio on the crowded freeway right before dawn my agent called, "Campbell, where are you?"

"On the freeway going to work, why?"

"Pull over immediately. Pull over, pull over, pull over!"

I do as she says, stopping in the nearest safe spot, "What is it, what's wrong?"

"It's your brother, the police just called."

"On no, what's he done? Where is he? I'll go get him."

"No, you don't understand. They need you to identify his body."

A huge lump stuck in my throat, and I started crying. Choked up, I raced across town to his place, parked behind the police car, and ran into the house where the coroner and two officers were waiting for me.

"Your brother was found in the bathroom" the only room I didn't check, "and we think he's been dead for two days," said the coroner. Then he took me in to see my brother decaying on the floor. It was an awful sight, one that still haunts me today.

I identified Matthew, then collapsed on the couch in tears as they took his body away. I had to call our mother to tell her she'd lost her child. No parent should ever go through that. I waited a few hours because of the time difference, but when she answered the phone she already knew. They were so connected that he'd already gotten the message to her. The time of death the coroner decided on was only about ten minutes before my mother's first call two days earlier.

AM: *What was the first hint you had of him being around you after that?*

Campbell: Making the funeral arrangements. My mother was really upset we couldn't get in touch with all his dancing friends from Vegas, Reno, San Francisco, and LA. It was hard trying to contact them all so quickly, but I knew they'll all come because in my mind I could hear Matthew saying, "Don't worry. They'll be there." Of course, I didn't tell mom that, I just reassured her that everything was under control. Sure enough, somehow he made sure the message got out, and his funeral was jam-packed.

Matthew always told me I should work with Cher. A week after the funeral, my agency got a call from her production team saying they wanted to try me out for a TV show she was doing. We got on great together, and I ended up doing the show with her, which I'm sure was his doing.

A few months later I broke up with my girl, the one Matthew said I had to call him about if was going to marry. She'd already partially moved to New York but was back in town for a week wrapping up the last of her life in LA. Since we weren't together anymore she stayed in the spare room, which is also where all Matthew's stuff was. In the morning she said she couldn't stay another night because Matthew's stuff was literally moving around in the room, and she kept hearing him say, "Get the fuck out!"

She went to stay with some other friends, leaving me wondering why Matthew was so angry with her. I told my housekeeper what happened and asked if she had any idea. At first, she was really embarrassed and didn't want to say anything, but I could see she knew something, so I really pushed her. Finally, she said that whenever I'd travel for work, that girl would bring other guys back to the house and have sex with them. Of course that's why Matthew wanted her out so badly. I started crying, not for the pain of her betrayal, but for the joy of realizing my brother's love and care. I ask why neither of them said anything. She said she didn't want to lose her job, and Matthew was sure I'd jump to the girl's defense. Of course, he was right, that's exactly what I'd have done.

AM: *What an awesome brother. Did he come through stronger after that?*

Campbell: Yes Matthew really started coming through powerfully when I met Teresa, a psychic from England. She knew nothing about me when we first sat down together, and immediately she said, "There's someone in the room with you. He's very tall and handsome, sort of like Brad Pitt, but he seems to be a dancer. I keep hearing Matt, Matt, like my son's name, Matthew."

The first thing I asked was why he didn't warn me about the girl, and immediately he replied, "You didn't need to know unless you were going to marry her. Now that she's gone you mustn't waste another moment of thought on her, you have far more important things to focus on. You're going to be connected to some completely new clients in Asia, open a new salon, and put out a range of products. I'll be there with you, so don't worry. Just keep doing what you're doing."

AM: *So Teresa really allowed the bridge between the two of you to be rebuilt?*

Campbell: Yes, connecting with him through her was how my own spiritual evolution began. His death was a rebirth for him, but it was a rebirth for me, too. I embraced spirituality with an open heart and let it cleanse my soul. Not only has he been my guide, but he's also connected me to my teachers.

AM: *So as time progressed has Matthew stayed with you, or did he help set you on your spiritual path and leave you to get on with it?*

Campbell: About three years ago, I was feeling that he wasn't around as much so I went for a reading with Teresa, and the first thing she said was, "Matthew knows you think he's not around anymore, and you're right. He's going off on his own now because he's done what he needs to do for you. It's time for you to let him go, but know that he'll be back."

Hearing that was a real relief, and allowed me to let him go knowing he's doing what he needs to. For the last few years I haven't felt him around at all, yet last Christmas he reappeared when I was at my parents' house in Sydney. My mom had been having some health issues, and we'd all been worried about her, but one evening I suddenly saw a little flash of blue light and felt him in my heart. Honestly, it was the best Christmas gift imaginable knowing he was back and that he was going to be there watching over her.

AM: *That's a great story. Thank you so much for sharing it so openly.*

Chapter 5

Starlette Young

I connected to Starlette Young through a mutual friend who saw my Facebook post saying I was looking for people with extraordinary stories of Spirit. I interviewed her by phone from her home in Colorado.

AM: *Starlette, tell me about your first experiences with Spirit.*

Starlette: It started with my mother, who was clairvoyant. She was always predicting things that'd come true. When I was around eight or nine, we were out picking blueberries in the fields when she suddenly dropped her bucket and said her mother had died. She took us straight back to the car and headed home, but on the way we saw one of her brothers coming the other way, waving frantically. Mom stopped and he jumped out of his car, ran up to us, leant into the window and said, "I have some bad news."

Mom nodded, "Yeah, I know. Mom just died."

That was my first experience. After that she'd sometimes wake me up and warn me about things that were going to happen. Many years later I saw a psychic in Denver who was well known for helping the local police solve crimes. She explained that holes in the fabric of time open and you can get glimpses of the future, seemed like as good an explanation as any.

AM: *You inherited the gift from your mom, but you don't call yourself a psychic?*

Starlette: I'm certainly sensitive. I feel energies when I walk into a room: fear, sadness, pain, **or** I feel if bad things have happened there. I can't go into casinos because I feel the pain of people losing their homes and more. It makes me want to throw up.

AM: *Would you share your daughter's story with us?*

Starlette: Sure, it happened back when we were living in Mississippi. We went over to have lunch with my husband Bill's family, who lived a couple hundred miles away. They had a long history of polycystic kidney disease, and his mother had just started dialysis, so of course the main topic of conversation while we were there was the disease and its implications. After we left, Bill and I continued talking about it in the car when suddenly my two-and-a-half-year-old daughter, who was sitting in the backseat with my son, started talking in a language I didn't recognize. I turned around and asked what language it was. Without missing a beat she said it was Hindi.

I asked where she learned it, and she replied that it was the language she spoke in her last life. She told us how she grew up in a large and loving family, but they were very poor so they didn't have much to eat, and their house was made of mud bricks with a dirt floor. She was one of the youngest members of their family. Then she described the town where they lived in great detail. I wish I'd written it down as I don't remember the name of it now. Then she said not to worry about getting our family disease because she died of it when she was eight back then, so she won't die of it again.

This was all a bit too much for my husband Bill, he got really freaked out and asked me to make her stop. Of course, I wanted her to tell me everything she remembered and asked her more about it, but Bill got so flustered by it that he didn't realize he'd speeded up. Suddenly a siren went off behind us and we got pulled over. As the officer walked up to the window, she snapped out of her trance and asked him if he was going to arrest her daddy. He just gave him a ticket, but as soon as he walked away I asked her to continue with her story. She had no idea what I was talking about, she didn't remember any of it, and to this day has no recollection of anything she said on that drive home.

AM: *That certainly suggests our individual spirit can and does enter different lives. This is something that's come up many times in my research, so I'm inclined to believe this is pretty normal. Thank you for sharing your story.*

Chapter 6

ANNA MARSHALL

Anna Marshall, a healer who lives in Colorado, was introduced to me by Starlette.

AM: *Anna, how did your experience with Spirit begin?*

Anna: With my massage therapy practice twenty years ago. Initially, I wasn't convinced. However, through my training in many healing disciplines I kept seeing firsthand the power that Spirit has to heal on so many levels. That's when I decided to dedicate myself to working with it, learning to be a conduit, and allowing Spirit to work through me to heal and help others.

A little after that my father passed away, and there was an incident at our house that made me sure he'd returned. The dogs suddenly went berserk, barking incessantly at nothing. It really looked as if they were barking at someone the way they were jumping around. It was like they were playing with someone I couldn't see. The next day I contacted a psychic here in Colorado who's worked a lot with the Denver Police, and she told me that my dad had indeed come by to see the dogs. Another man came with him who looked almost like his twin. At first, I wasn't sure who it was, but then I realized it was my brother who passed away prematurely in 1960. I was shocked to realize that a spirit continues to grow and develop even if the life it was living was cut short.

AM: *Have you've had any other notable experiences with Spirit?*

Anna: It is so much a part of everything I do that it's hard for me to pull out specific things. In the last few days, I was thinking about you and how you'd wanted to talk to me, but I'd misplaced your phone number. I knew not to worry because if I think about someone they usually call within a day or two. I always know when a client needs to see me, and I believe things like that are both powerful and not random. I've always had the ability to know when someone was ill, and if they'd survive their illness. In the last couple months, I've started to hone my ability to know things and then help people I'm close to without them even being present.

On New Year's Eve I couldn't get a very close friend of the family off my mind. The feeling was so urgent and insistent that I was on the verge of panic. I knew something was very wrong, and I knew it was with his heart. I didn't want to frighten him, so I asked my aunt to give him a call and see how he was. It turned out his son had a heart attack that very evening. I'd picked up on the pain, but it was his son's condition.

AM: *When we first spoke, you mentioned you're aware of when people will pass.*

Anna: Yes, since I was a little girl. At first, I thought it a curse, but now I realize it's a gift, even if it isn't such a cheery one. Anyway, I've learned to live with it. I'm aware of how the energy around people changes as they get close to the veil between this dimension and the next. Moving from here to there isn't a bad thing. Take Star's husband, Bill. Before he passed over he kept questioning why he was still here, suffering from one health crisis to another. He just wanted to get to a place where everything was okay, so for him moving to the next dimension was a huge release. A big part of healing is helping people transition from here to there when it's their time to go.

AM: *Yes, in doing this book I've come to understand that for Spirit, death is indeed a rebirth into a higher dimension. Thank you for sharing your experience with us.*

Chapter 7

John Pearson

John Pearson is a world-renowned model, actor, and writer. He was also with me on one of my first trips to LA, when we were shooting a Ray-Ban campaign together.

AM: *John, tell us about your experience with Spirit?*

John: In June 1990 I was about to embark on the filmmakers intensive course at NYU. I'd just moved into a new apartment, and the night before my first day I was deeply concerned about my ability to grasp the complex technicalities that the course involved. I've never been a technical sort, but my father was an engineer so I hoped that somewhere in my DNA his ability is waiting to be awakened. If he were alive now, he'd be immersed in computers and the new electronic frontier, but he died in 1976 when he was just forty-five, and I was eleven.

So fourteen years later, there I am in my East Village apartment with butterflies in my stomach, and my mind full of self-doubt. I got to bed pretty early, hoping to get a good sleep, but I found it very difficult to switch off from the worrying that I wouldn't be up to the task. After tossing and turning for a while, I finally just said out loud, "Dad, I know you were really good at this. This was your world, but I'm very nervous. Please help me. Give me some sort of sign that I'll be able to cope."

I felt rather odd doing this, but did it nonetheless, and almost immediately I got the feeling of two warm hands gently taking each side of my head and nodding it twice. It was gentle, but definitive. I was totally startled, but at the same comforted by a wave of absolute love that washed through me. I knew it was his doing, and as I'd really wanted to reconnect with his spirit, it filled me with both joy and gratitude.

Sure enough, when I finally fell asleep, he came to me in my dreams. He was as vivid and clear as looking at you now, standing in beautiful, radiant health, serene, graceful. He was wearing a crisp white shirt and khaki shorts, and in profile about four feet away from me. We were on what looked like a wide, beautiful northeastern beach, and he was facing out to sea. He turned, looked at me, and our eyes met. In that moment, I felt totally connected, at one with him and everything else. Without him uttering a word, I heard the message in his eyes: "I'm right here with you, and you're going to be fine." Then he smiled a quiet smile, nodded twice, and was gone.

I awoke full of courage, energy, curiosity, and inspiration, knowing without question that he IS with me, a part of me, and in some way inseparable from me. I flew through the entire course brilliantly, loving every moment of it, and I came away having done better than I could ever have imagined.

AM: *That's such an inspiring and beautiful story. Thank you.*

Chapter 8

Desiree Kohan

Desiree Kohan owns and runs one of LA's chicest fashion boutiques where she has debuted many of Europe's hottest new designers before anyone else in the city even knew about them. Her store, Des Kohan, is at 671 S. Cloverdale Ave., Los Angeles 90036, and her website is www.deskohan.com.

AM: *Desiree, would you please tell us the story of your grandmother?*

Desiree: She'd been in a steep descent for a couple of months, and when she finally went into the hospital, everyone in our family knew it was time. She was rushed straight into the intensive care unit, and put in a bed unconscious with IVs in her arms and tubes down her throat. Everyone in our family took turns standing vigil, but my brother and I were there the most. After four days of being in a coma she started to come to, so we called the family and told everyone to come right away. They arrived within an hour, my parents, uncles, aunts, and all of us grandkids crammed into her little hospital room, when suddenly she woke up.

At this point, she'd been deathly ill for two months and hadn't eaten for four days or more, but the first thing she said was, "I've never had so much energy in my life." Her voice was clear and bright, almost as if she was speaking with a microphone. She told us she'd been looking down on earth from above, where she'd been charged with light and love. Everything is love, it's the energy and fabric of creation. It's what we come from, it's what we'll return to, and it's indescribably beautiful. However, she also had a warning for us: the energy of the world is changing, and evil is taking over. She told us that the people in power have become completely corrupted, and have turned away from the light. A very dark time is coming, and to survive it, our family must bond together tightly. Our union must be rock solid. We're to stay close together, look out for one another, and stick to our morals and values. This really shocked us because she'd always been both devoutly religious and incredibly positive, but now she was warning us about a period of great global evil.

Next, she spoke to each of us, one by one. First she acknowledged our unique spirit and described our missions here on earth. She told one of my cousins that he's to be the center of the family, and that he came here to bring us light and love. She praised all he'd done for us and said that she blesses him. She spoke to everyone and finished by telling each of us how much she loved us. It was like she'd downloaded everyone's mission here on **earth, and** wanted to praise all the beautiful and kind things they've done. Then she looked at my brother and me and said, "Don't think I didn't notice you here just because my eyes were closed. I want you to know I saw you and Nouriel every minute, and I love you both."

We were all shocked someone who'd been gravely ill for months spoke with so much vigor. It was as if she'd come back to give everyone her warning, her words of wisdom, and her blessings. After that she gently slipped back to sleep, then into her coma, and within the week she'd passed over.

AM: *What a wonderful story, although her warning about the great evil that is taking over the world certainly should give us all pause for concern.*

Chapter 9

Omar Albertto

I met Omar Albertto when I first came to LA in the late eighties. He was running Omar's Men, one of the most successful modeling agencies in Los Angeles. Today, he's running JustOmar, a full branding and management company with offices in Los Angeles and Panama, and remains one of LA's most iconic and popular entrepreneurs.

AM: *Omar, thanks for agreeing to share you your story with us. What do you remember about it, and how it happened?*

Omar: I was always very close to my mother. Even though she lived in Panama we were so connected that if I'd thought of her, right away the phone would ring, or if she'd thought of me, vice versa. The day she traveled, I like to call it traveling, not dying, I was at home in Los Angeles. Suddenly, in the middle of doing my sit-ups, my body just froze, I literally couldn't move a muscle. I found myself staring at the digital clock on the VCR, which read 11:11.

Sandro, my son, looked at me and asked, "Dad, are you all right?"

I couldn't even breathe to answer him because deep inside I knew something terrible had happened. As quickly as it came, the sudden paralysis went. I jumped up, grabbed the phone, and called Panama. Nobody answered. There's always someone there, my mom, dad, or our housekeeper, so I knew it was bad. I kept calling and calling until eventually Braulia, our housekeeper, answered. I could hear in the tone of her voice that something was really wrong.

"Where's Mom?" I asked.

"Señor Omar, I'm so sorry, but she died a few hours ago."

It turned out that she traveled at exactly 1:11pm, or 11:11am here in Los Angeles.

Years before I remember telling my mother how when people pass over here in the United States, they leave behind lots of money for their relatives. She was very proud, and immediately she said she'd make sure our family would have a good inheritance when she died too. I told her I'd always keep the house because she'd worked so hard for so long to give us such a beautiful home, and now it was part of our family heritage.

When I flew down to Panama for the funeral, I went straight to the house. I arrived around 9:30 p.m, and a family gathering was planned for later that night. Of course everyone wanted to know how things were going to be resolved. I'd left LA with so much on my plate that I went straight up to my room and got on the phone to take care of business back there.

My brother arrived from New Jersey a little later, and rushed straight upstairs and barged into my room while I was still on the phone. We didn't have the best relationship when Mom was alive because he never treated her with the love and respect she deserved, which really annoyed me. However, both he and my sister weren't doing so well financially, so I knew he'd be leaning on me to sell the house.

Without even saying hello he told me to get off the phone because we have things to discuss. I ignored him because I knew all he wanted to talk about was selling the house and when he'd get his money. I had no intention of entertaining that conversation as I'd already made up my mind we were keeping it. He stood there glaring at me, so I said, "Can't you see I'm on the phone? I'll be with you when everyone else gets here."

He slunk out of the room and I returned to my work calls. When they were finally done, I took a deep breath and went back downstairs to meet the gathering of the vultures on the patio. Everyone knew I wasn't selling the house, and that my brother and I were going to have a battle royal over it, but I didn't care. I loved that house, it was our heritage, our home and my last connection to my mother. We were keeping it, and that was final. I'd take care of my sister, she's my life, but my brother could go fuck himself.

As I walked past the kitchen door, the digital clock on the stove caught my eye, and stopped me in my tracks. It read 11:11. Then as clear as day I heard my mother's voice right inside my head as if I'm wearing headphones, "Baby, don't do this. Don't fight with your brother. Please sell the house."

In that moment she changed my mind. I walked onto the patio with everyone's eyes on me, and my brother seething. Our housekeeper, Braulia, looked at me as if she had something to say, but with tears in my eyes, I put my hand up to stop her. Placing my other hand on my heart, I said, "We're going to sell the house."

Braulia said, "Oh, Señor Omar, I'm so happy you said that. That's the last thing your mother told me, she really wanted you to sell the house."

Ever since that day, 11:11 is my time with Mother. I even have 11:11 tattooed on my arm. We speak often, sometimes twice a day. Everyone who knows me well knows that wherever I am and whatever I'm doing, I'll stop for that one minute to be with my mother. Last year she was really mad at me because she didn't like the woman I was dating. Every time 11:11 came round I'd hear her telling me to get out. It was hard because I hate confrontations, making waves, or having bad vibes, and I'd developed a strong bond with this woman's kids. I couldn't figure out how to get out cleanly, but Mom kept pushing and pushing. Eventually, I discovered why. It's enough to say it was both really ugly and painful. Of course, my mom knew best. She had been trying to protect me for the whole year.

AM: *So your mom really helped you get out of it?*

Omar: She did. I couldn't stand having her mad at me, and I knew she was really angry about that. She was pounding me, begging me, and telling me daily to get away from the relationship. She kept letting me know that woman wasn't good for me, and that she'd take me down. You know what? She was quite right, she almost did.

AM: *Since getting out of that, do you still feel your mom around?*

Omar: Every day I have these incredible one-minute conversations with her. Does she always reply to me? Absolutely not. Do I feel her presence? Absolutely. Does she make sure I notice whenever our time comes up? Always. I know at 11:11 every day, sometimes twice a day, that her traveling has not separated us. Quite the reverse, it made us inseparable. The bond of our love was and always will be incredible. It grows stronger and stronger with each passing day.

My brother's changed, too. He's become the most wonderful man, friend, and brother. We've become the loving family that my mother always wanted us to be, because love really is all we have that's worth having.

AM: *What a great story. Thank you for sharing it.*

Chapter 10

KAREN KAWAHARA

Karen Kawahara is a celebrated makeup artist who's work has graced many famous faces over the last twenty years. Recently she's worked on *Curb Your Enthusiasm*, *The New Adventures of Old Christine*, *Better with You*, *Veep*, and *The Exes*.

I first met Karen on a cover shoot for *In Style* magazine and have a vivid memory of coming into the makeup room to see her using a Ouija board with our celebrity of the day. I'd always wanted to chat about it more then, but in the pressure cooker of our work days I never had the opportunity, so I'm happy to finally be able to ask her about it here.

AM: *Who was Fred, and how did he come into your life?*

Karen: Fred was my best friend, he was more than just my best friend, he was like my brother. We were so close that we both believed we were together in a past life.

In the mid-eighties, he was diagnosed with AIDS, which was a death sentence in those days. As the disease progressed, he went into hospital and quickly deteriorated. I'd visit him as often as I could, and one afternoon while he was slipping in and out of consciousness, he said, "If there's any way I can come back, I will. He passed a few days later, just a couple weeks before Thanksgiving. I knew he'd been trying to hang on to share it with all his friends one last time, but his body just couldn't make it.

We all went to his funeral, and tried hard to celebrate his life while hiding our sadness. Then it was Thanksgiving. I always had loads of friends over, as most of us didn't have any family in LA, so we were a family of friends. Fred would always be with us, and everyone was missing him badly, so we set a place for him at the table.

One of our friends brought a large box of cream-topped cupcakes from our favorite local bakery, Sweet Lady Jane. We opened it, admiring the exquisite icing, but there was no room in the fridge so I resealed the box and put it out on the garden porch since it was such a cold day. We ate our turkey dinner, and when it came to dessert, I brought in the box, put it on the table, and opened it. Everybody gasped. The cupcakes all had finger marks in them, as if somebody had scooped up the icing with their fingers. My first thought was that it was Fred, because he had the biggest sweet tooth ever, then suddenly all the ornamental baskets I had hanging on the wall flew off into the room. No one flinched, and my daughters both said, "Mom, look, it's uncle Fred!"

I laughed, but inside I felt a little uneasy. Everyone agreed we should toast him, so we raised our glasses, thanked him for coming, and wished him a Happy Thanksgiving.

After the party died down and everyone left, I hung the baskets back on the wall. As I did I examined the hooks and nails they were hanging on to rationalize how they'd all flown off like that, but they were all perfectly in place. In the following weeks, lights randomly started going on and off on their own, and I'd find odd things moved from one place to another, so I had a sense, or maybe a hope, that he was there.

Shortly after the holidays, we moved into a new house. I had no sense of Fred being around until one day I heard my five-year-old daughter talking to someone in her bedroom. I knew we were alone in the house, so I went up to her room to see who was there with her. As I opened the door I saw her sitting on her bed, giggling, so I glanced around the room, but there wasn't anybody there. Suddenly, she said, "Oh Fred, stop it."

"What's going on?" I asked.

"Look, Mom! Uncle Fred's playing with the light in the closet!"

I looked, and sure enough, the little chain on the light switch pulled down on its own, and the light turned on with a click. It pulled down again, and the light turned off with another click.

"Can you see him?" I asked.

"Yes, he's right there!" she said, pointing at the empty space below the chain.

I believed her because I really wanted him to be there, but it was hard not being able to see him. I was both happy and concerned, but most of all, I wanted to make sure this was safe for the girls. I asked some friends about it, and one suggested I go to see a well-known and respected medium living in Hollywood. I phoned and made an appointment. He instructed me that the night before I see him, I should think of the spirits I want to come, light a candle, and say a prayer because when you focus on them it helps call them in.

On the way to see him, I couldn't help feeling a bit skeptical, so I decided not to tell him anything about myself except my name. When we sat in session the first person who came through was my grandmother, a glamorous and strong New Yorker of German descent who used to take me shopping as a kid. She mentioned the house at the lake where we spent our summers. Then the medium told me an older gentleman was there too, standing right behind her. He was saying "pinchy, pinchy" and pinching his cheeks. I knew it was my grandfather, I used to call him Pinchy Papa because he always used to pinch my cheeks. There's no way the medium could ever have known all of that, so I knew he was for real. Then he said, "There's someone else here. He says you were with him when he passed, and he was very scared."

I knew it was Fred because he asked me if he was dying. I told him he was because we had a pact never to lie to each other. Then he asked me for morphine for the pain, so I got the nurse to give it to him to help him pass over. She did, and I held his hand as he slipped away. He looked up at me and asked, "Are you going to be okay?"

"Yes," I replied.

"Okay. Well, I'm going to go now, and I'll wait for you on the other side," he said, closing his eyes. I held his hand as he crossed over, but I always worried about telling him the truth that day and thought maybe I shouldn't have.

The medium continued, "He says he was scared, but he's really happy you didn't lie to him. He knew it was time and was so happy that you were there with him. He wants you to know he loves you."

I left there relieved and happy knowing Fred was okay on the other side, and thought no more about it, until a few months later when I was on location shooting a movie. An actress I was working with suggested a group of us try the Ouija board after work. I'd never done it before, but was happy to go along with the idea as everyone else was so excited by it. At first not much happened, but then the glass started moving around like crazy. Letter by letter it spelt out, "Hi Karen."

"Who's there?" I replied.

"It's Fred," the glass spells.

"Fred who?" I asked, and fast as lightning, he spells out his full name: Fred Mamaraldo. I gasped, then explained to everyone that he was my best friend who'd passed the year before. He told me he loved me and to tell the girls hi. Suddenly, everyone wanted to ask him questions, and Fred answered them. He did it so quickly that someone had to write down what he was spelling out to make the sentences. I don't know how he was predicting all these things, but he really knew what was going to happen.

That was how it began, and before long everyone I was working with wanted to speak to Fred. I can't give you their names because they're all celebrities, but as you know I took the board with me on all my jobs, and he helped a lot of people. He even helped one actress I worked with negotiate a contract for a show! He told another that there was a baby boy with him, and he'd be coming next year. A year later, we met again on a different film, and she asked to speak to Fred. The first thing he said is "What about the baby boy?" We looked at each other, and I asked if she's pregnant. Shyly, she said yes, but made me swear not to tell anyone as she's Jewish, and in her faith you mustn't say anything about it until after the first three months. Of course I agreed, and we giggled about Fred ratting her out. Eight months later, she had a little boy.

Another actress kept asking him the same question over and over each time we did a session, but she worded it differently, until Fred said, "Listen, it doesn't matter how many times you ask, the answer isn't going to change."

He told another actress she'd adopt a child in a few years and even gave the little boy's name. Sure enough, five years later, I saw the story in *People* magazine. Fred's sense of humor and fun never changed, and much to all our amusement, he'd always flirt with any cute guys who came to the board. He predicted so many things, including Emmy and Oscar nominations, which were always right.

Everyone in my circle of friends and associates who'd doubted Spirit before, doesn't anymore. Even my second husband, a dentist with a scientist's brain, wasn't initially a believer, but now he is.

We've since moved to the East Coast, and Fred doesn't come around as much anymore. The last time I saw him was in a dream that was so real I could even smell him. We were laughing and talking as we walked down a huge spiral ramp in the sky. It was so good to be together again, to see him so happy and healthy. Then he told me he couldn't go any farther, he had to stop there. I told him I got it, then he said he'll see me soon and waved as I walked on down the ramp alone. I woke up filled with joy.

Fred's completely removed my fear of dying. I know I'm going to see him, and everyone else I love, again.

AM: *That really does sound like the most incredible life-changing experience. Have you done anything with what you've learned from your experiences with Fred?*

Karen: Yes, I volunteered at an AIDS hospice and helped a lot of people pass over. I always felt it to be the best way of sharing Fred's gift—letting people approaching the end here know that they're going on to something so beautiful. Through his love, I'm able to make them laugh and take care of them until they're safely on the other side.

AM: *That is one of the most inspiring things I've heard. It would be so wonderful to know we all have someone to help us make that final step when our time comes. Thank you for sharing your story.*

Chapter 11

DAWN BAILLIE

Dawn Baillie is a native of Los Angeles and one of the founding partners of BLT, an exceptionally successful film, TV, and theatrical advertising agency in Los Angeles.

AM: *Thanks for being a part of the book and sharing your stories of Spirit. How did it start for you?*

Dawn: I was quite young, around ten. My grandmother was in an assisted-living home and in failing health, so I knew she wasn't going to be with us for much longer. Late one afternoon while I was walking around the neighborhood's quiet little streets with Rufus, our family pit bull, I suddenly saw her coming toward us. She looked just like she always did, but somehow even more serene and peaceful. She had the palms of her hands open, facing us, but then I realized she didn't have any feet! She was just floating toward us slightly above the ground. Rufus barked frantically, turned, and dragged me away. We sprinted back to the house as fast as we could, bolted up the stairs to my bedroom and locked the door. I couldn't make sense of what we'd just seen, but I could see Rufus was still really troubled.

About fifteen minutes later the phone rang downstairs, so I opened my door and listened as my Mom answered it. I could tell by her tone something bad had happened, so I went back down the stairs as she put it down. She looked at me, and before she could say anything, I said, "Grandma died." She nodded and we hugged each other, but inside I had a terrible sense of guilt. I felt like the image was something I'd created in my mind, but in doing so was responsible for her death.

AM: *Did she appear to you again?*

Dawn: Not like that, no, but I'd feel her sitting at the foot of my bed for about a year afterward.

AM: *Have you had any other experiences with Spirit?*

Dawn: A few brief ones from time to time, glimpses of things that have made me sure there's much more to this reality than we know, but the next major one was after a friend of mine's son died in a tragic accident. She desperately wanted to connect with him, and after hearing a bout the renowned local medium, Hollister Rand, she asked me if I'd go with her. I'd seen Hollister give a demonstration a few years earlier, so I agreed, hoping she'd help my friend connect with her son. I brought my mom, too, and we all went to the old Bodhi Tree bookstore where Hollister was doing her demonstration. During it, she asked if anyone had a black cat on the other side, my mom said yes. The cat came with a large woman who was unquestionably my grandmother. She'd come with a message for my mom to mind her own business and stay out our other family's dealings, which proved to be very timely.

Later that night, just as I got into bed and closed my eyes, a spirit of some kind got caught between my eyelids and reality. As I shut my eyes I saw leaves gathering right in front of me. I couldn't help being shocked at how hyperreal and super sharp they were as they swirled into the shape of a face with hollow eyes and a mouth. I could feel them too, as if they were right inside my eyelids. A deep masculine voice started speaking in a language I didn't understand. I was terrified, and just managed to get out the words, "I don't know what you're saying, and I don't want to hear it. Please go!"

Then I opened my eyes. The leaves instantly become an inverted-color image of the same face, like a photographic negative. The voice got louder, so I closed my eyes again. The leaf face inverted. I opened them again, and it flipped again. Panicked I opened and closed my eyes frantically, trying to get rid of it, but it just kept jumping from negative to positive. Finally I sat up in bed, and burst right through the leaves.

I really focused on pushing the image and the voice away, and then they were gone. With a deep sigh of relief, I lay back down thinking it was done, but as my head hit the pillow the leaves rushed back into my eyes, making that face again.

Heart palpitating, I sat back up, and they scattered again. I laid back down, and the leaves rushed back in. The voice came again, louder. I closed my eyes, but the image just inverted. I couldn't get rid of it, and I was completely terrified, so I started reciting a mantra that my spiritual teacher in India had given me. As I repeated it over and over, two fine cones of light gathered at my bedroom door. They were very slender shapes yet oddly humanlike at the same time. One of them lifted up its arms which silenced the voice and scattered the leaves. A wave of relief washed over me, and I thanked the two light forms. The way they cleared the room and changed the energy left me feeling deeply and beautifully connected to the world and Spirit.

AM: *Do you have any sense of what it was?*

Dawn: I think it was some sort of spirit hitchhiker that was attracted by Hollister's channeling and latched on to me, but I wasn't able to detect it, nor could it work it's mischief, until the moments of stillness right before sleep. The funny thing is my mother had a very similar experience that night, so there was definitely something in the air.

AM: Thank you for sharing your stories and introducing me to Hollister Rand. I've since done several workshops with her, and she has given us some incredible insights in the next section.

Chapter 12

Tiffany Saidnia and Pegah Anvarian

Tiffany Saidnia and Pegah Anvarian are both fashion designers. At the time of this story, they were working together on the launch of one of Pegah's first collections. This interview with both of them was recorded at my home in LA.

AM: *Tiffany, tell us what you both remember of the evening in Pegah's old studio.*

Tiffany: It happened about two weeks into my working for Pegah, and about thirteen months after my father's passing. He was sixty-two when he was struck with something that seemed like a stroke. He went to the hospital, where the doctors initially thought he was fine, but he suddenly fell into an unexplained coma. After a few weeks with no turn-around, his body started to fail really badly, and we had no choice but to pull the plug. I was twenty-two, my brother was twenty-six, and my mother was in her late forties. It was such a shock that the entire family was still a total mess a year later. None of them had begun healing or had recovered from his loss except for me because I'd felt him around me, in the house, and in the car, too. It was so real that I honestly felt like he was still with me, and I hadn't lost him after all. Pegah also said she'd gotten a strong sense of him a few times when we were together.

The night before I was at the opening of the Bvlgari store on Rodeo Drive, where they had a psychic giving readings. I sat with her hoping to hear something lovely from my father, but instead she told me all the awful things about him and myself that were both very hurtful and unsettling.

As soon as I got to work, I told Pegah about the reading because it had kept me awake all night, and I was still really upset about it. That's when Pegah told me that she's psychic. Honestly I just laughed and thought nothing more of it. Anyhow, the day passed normally, but as the sun set an incredibly strong scent of cologne overtook the little studio. I asked Pegah if she smelled it, and she did. We thought that it must be coming from the hallway, so we opened the door and poked our heads out, but there was no smell in the corridor at all.

"This is too weird. Maybe it's Keith in the office next door. I'll go ask him," I said, and went to knock on his door as Pegah went back into our office.

"Keith, there's a really strong smell of cologne in our office. You didn't break a bottle of it in here, did you?" I asked.

"No, I never wear the stuff. I don't even like it." he replied.

"Okay. Never mind. Thanks," I said, and returned to our studio. Right away, Pegah asked me if it's my father's scent, but my mother was allergic to all kinds of perfumes and colognes, so I'd never associated any scent with him. Then Pegah just said, "Your father's here, and he wants to talk to you."

The power of the scent and the clarity of Pegah's voice somehow made me sure this was real, even though it didn't make sense.

AM: *Pegah, what happened when Tiffany was out of the room?*

Pegah: It was late, around seven-thirty or eight, and everyone had already left for the day, so it was just us. The power of the scent got crazy strong again right as Tiffany came back into the studio, and then out of nowhere I was hit with an overwhelming desire to talk really fast without having anything to say. I picked up a pen and start drawing with an incredible sense of urgency. Honestly, I don't really like tuning into Spirit, it's something I try to keep at arm's length because it can be very draining, but his presence was so strong that I knew I had to do it.

AM: *So what happened next?*

Tiffany: Pegah said, "He wants to talk to you." Then she said all these things that absolutely validated it was him, like, "I know when you wore my watch after I gave it to you," and "Your mother's just worn red nail polish for the first time since I left because she's been in mourning, wearing all those horrible dark colors for a year. It's time to wear bright colors again, you know I love bright and happy colors." Pegah used the Persian word *shadpousha*, which means "bright and happy." It's not a word that people typically use, but it's a word my father always used. Pegah doesn't speak Pharsi that well and was saying things I knew she didn't understand, so there was no question that it was him speaking through her.

He continued, "I am in the house with you all, but you're the only one who feels me. I'm with you in the car when you start crying. Your mother needs to believe and know I'm still here with you, and I'm staying around to look after you all because everyone's so unsettled. I want to bring you all peace. You have to tell your brother and mother that they need to know and believe that I'm there with them,"

"How did you die?" I asked. Even though thirteen specialists were looking after him at Cedars-Sinai hospital, none of them had been able to identify what killed him. "I ate something traveling on business that had some form of parasite in it," he replied. The parasite started eating away at his body. He said it's something that more people are going to get, a form of mad-cow disease. Whatever it was, it visibly ate away at his skin and his body just shut down.

Pegah: I said all that to you? Oh my goodness!

Tiffany: Uh, huh.

Pegah: And you remember all this?

Tiffany: Of course I do! My father came back to speak to me from the dead, I'm gonna remember what he had to say!

Pegah: This is fascinating, I really don't remember any of it!

Tiffany: I know, you were like a medium, which is what you are, and you weren't processing any of it. Like you said, you just wanted to get the words out.

Pegah: Okay, what else did he say?

Tiffany: He asked me to ask him questions.

Pegah: So what did you ask him?

Tiffany: How I'll do in business. He said, "Just fine." Then I asked when I'd find love and get married. He laughed and said, "It'll come." Then he told me not to go to any more psychics or readers and that if I did, he'd be angry with me. He said if I have any questions like that, I'm to ask him, and he'll get me the answers.

AM: *In the ten years since, have you asked him questions and found the answers?*

Tiffany: Well, at the end of my last relationship, I really needed an answer or a sign from him, so I begged him for his help. I do think he gave me a sign because I felt his presence.

AM: *How do you feel he gave you the sign?*

Tiffany: By my ex's actions. He acted so illogically and so out of character that it was as if he had been pushed away. It was all so sudden.

Pegah: I feel like because you asked from such a deep part of your soul and you wanted the answer so badly that maybe you rushed what would have taken much longer to happen. You pushed fast-forward, which is why your answer was so sudden and final.

AM: *Did you feel him around you again after that time?*

Tiffany: One night, I woke up and saw him lying on the bed next to me. His eyes were open wide in the shock and disbelief that I could see him.

You know there's something very sad about losing a father at such a young age. He was so incredibly proud of me and he gave me my self-confidence. I remember going to China for work, felling really proud of myself for getting that contract, but it was hard not having my biggest cheerleader to share it with. Whenever I get really excited about work, I start crying because he's missing it. Once when I was crying, I heard a loud crash in the next room. I went in the other room, and nothing had fallen. I never did find out what it was, but now I'm certain it was him telling me to stop crying.

Pegah: I remember that he said he moved a piece of furniture, too, a bed or sofa, and he told you the direction it moved.

AM: *Pegah, do you remember the whole conversation like he was in the room?*

Pegah: Not really. I get it through a feeling and then translate it into words, but sometimes like with Tiffany's dad, the words just sort of flow through me. Sometimes I do hear the spirits, but it honestly it makes me pretty uneasy and even a little scared, which throws me off from being able to do the reading. I think they communicate to me through feeling first because I'm so sensitive to that. I have to be really open and let the feelings and the energy flow through me, and I often have to do something like drawing to occupy my mind while I'm channeling.

AM: *That's a great story. Thank you both so much for sharing it.*

Chapter 13

Scott Nathan

Scott Nathan is a photographer working in LA who I met through mutual friends. When he heard about my project, he told me about his first experience with Carissa Schumacher, a powerful medium who lives and works in the Laguna Mountains in Southern California. His tale is a wonderful example of how Spirit can heal the past.

AM: *What happened when you first phoned Carissa?*

Scott: I didn't ask her anything, and she had no backstory on me other than what I did and where I lived. Immediately she said, "You're looking for your biological father."

"Yes, I am," I replied, "And I've just hired my third private investigator in a decade to try to find him,"

"Well, he's here with me now," she said.

"What do mean, he's with you now?"

"I'm sorry to tell you, but he passed away two years ago. He says he's really sorry he wasn't there for you."

"What else?"

"His name is Joe Harris, and he lived in Pennsylvania. He wants you to know you have a half sibling from a British woman who lives in Los Angeles, and you also have a brother and a sister in New York from another marriage."

Right after getting off the phone with her, I called the private investigator and ask him to track down Joe Harris, who I think is deceased, in Pennsylvania. Of course he asked how I suddenly knew all this, so I tell him it's just a hunch. Anyhow, he gets back to me a couple of days later with two numbers. I called the first one, but the deep African-American voice who answered is obviously not my dad, so I try the second one. A woman answered.

"Is this Joe Harris's house?" I asked.

"Yes, but you're a little late. He died two years ago. Who is this?" she replied.

"Before I tell you, let me clear up a few things. Did he live in Los Angeles in the sixties?"

"Yes."

"And in Chicago in '64?"

"Yes."

"And he worked in the insurance business?"

"Yes."

"Well, I'm his son!"

"Not another one!"

"What's that supposed to mean?" I ask.

"He had three other kids, and they all just met at his funeral for the first time."

Carissa was spot on! So I met my sister in LA first, and it turned out she lived just around the corner from me, too. She's an Orthodox Jew and a really sweet lady. I figured I'd meet the other two next time I was in New York, but my newly found New York sister called me up saying she was coming to LA and would be staying with her childhood best friend, who, by an even crazier coincidence, turned out to be my ex-girlfriend's mother! So now I've met both my sisters. My Orthodox sister decided to arrange a meal for us all, finally all four of his kids got to break bread together.

AM: *So how did you get to be number four?*

Scott: He married four times. My two New York siblings are from his first marriage. I was the result of a short affair during his third marriage. My LA sister is from the third marriage and is only a couple of months older than me. So he'd gotten her mother, his British wife, pregnant, and they went back to London to give birth under the socialized medicine. He went back to Chicago on business while she was in London, and that's when he had the affair with my mother and got her pregnant. His third wife had the baby in London, then they moved back to Chicago.

It was shortly after that my mom's father knocked on his door, and said, "You got my daughter pregnant. What are you going to do about it?" Wife number three heard the whole thing and split to LA, so I had a sister and her mother here the whole time!

AM: *What happened to your dad after that?*

Scott: He married that woman I spoke to in Pensilvania and stayed with her for thirty-five years, but they never had any children. She was really sweet and sent me loads of pictures of him. I guess he was just a lovable fuck-up, a charming and charismatic guy who couldn't keep his rocket in his pocket.

AM: *What a great story, and thank you for introducing me to Carissa, she really has an amazing gift and has given us some incredible insights in the next section.*

Chapter 14

Valerie Jean Garduno

I first met Valerie Jean Garduno at Heathrow Airport, when we were about to fly out to Ethiopia together on a location shoot for British *Elle*. For both of us, the trip to that magical country was one of the more memorable experiences of our time in fashion. We lost touch for almost twenty years until we happened to run into each other while walking our dogs in LA's Griffith Park about a month after I started working on this book. People pop up again at the most opportune times, and her story also demonstrates the power that Spirit has, to affect life for the better when channeled through a bona fide medium.

AM: *How did you first hear about Jeffrey Wands?*

Valerie Jean: My mom told me about him. She told me that he's a really great medium and seer, so I called up for an appointment. At that time, the wait was almost a year and a half, so that's quite a build up!

AM: *What was your first impression of him?*

Valerie Jean: I remember being surprised by how brief and to the point he was. Of course the reading resonated with me, which is why I've gone back to him several times over the last fourteen years.

AM: *Has he told you things that have changed your life?*

Valerie Jean: Yes. My parents separated when I was just a year old, and I was brought up by my mother. My father wasn't a great dad, nor was he really a part of my childhood. In my adult life I saw him infrequently, and when I did, it was never deep, meaningful, or emotionally fulfilling. When I eventually saw Jeffrey, he told me to write a letter to my father and tell him everything I've ever wanted to, the good and the bad, the disappointments, the sadnesses, the great memories, and the things I love about him. He told me not to send it, but to go to Colorado right away, take him out to breakfast, and read him the letter. I asked if I couldn't just send it, but Jeffrey was insistent, it must be read in person. I mentioned I was going to Colorado in three weeks, and he said do it then, but it absolutely has to be then and no later. He also reiterated that I have to take him out to breakfast and read it to him.

Writing my dad a letter and taking him to breakfast are both things I'd never considered doing, but I spent much of the three weeks prior to my trip working on it. As soon as I got to Colorado, I took him out to breakfast and, as instructed, read him the letter. It was really cathartic, we cried, we laughed, and the whole experience completely cleared the energy between us. After breakfast we hugged and said good-bye, then as I watched him walk back to his car, I felt truly at peace with him for the first time ever.

A couple of weeks later, without any warning, he passed away of a sudden illness. If Jeffrey hadn't been so adamant about it, I'd never have had closure and always would have regretted not saying those things to him. He knew something was up and knew what I had to do for me. I don't say so much that he knew, but the spirits who he was channeling knew, and he made sure I got their message.

AM: *That's a great story. Thank you for sharing and introducing me to Jeffrey. He's also agreed to be in our panel of experts in the next section.*

Chapter 15

Hope Rechea

I connected with Hope Rechea through Valerie Jean, who'd known her in NYC. I was really struck by the drama and courage of Hope's tale. While completely different from Claudia's story, it echoes certain elements of it and really opens our minds to what it means to totally surrender to Spirit. This is a very abridged version of her story, which was given to me over two phone interviews and it's also the basis for her own novel, *Illusions of a Love Story*.

AM: *Hope, how did your experience with Spirit begin?*

Hope: I could see and feel things as a child, but my mother was adamant that I was just imagining things, so for a long time I really didn't pay it any attention. I did what you're meant to do: I grew up, found a great man, got married, had a family, and became a soccer mom. Life was great, I was living the American dream, and everything was exactly as it should be. Then bang! The floodgates opened, and I started knowing things. Guides, guidance, voices in my head, call it what you will, but they were telling me things that would happen to people. And they did happen. Living in super-conventional, Republican, Bible Belt North Carolina, where people are inclined to either say it's the devil's work or that you're going crazy, gave me good reason to be cautious and concerned about what was happening to me. I started sharing it with a few trusted friends, and before long, people were coming to me for guidance. It really proved itself over and over again. I really could help people through being able to see what was going to happen in their lives, so I learned to trust it.

Well, it wouldn't have been so bad if it had stopped there, but it didn't. The same guidance started demanding that I give up everything. It said I had to leave my family and friends to go on a spiritual pilgrimage to India, where I would learn to heal. This went on for months, but I kept suppressing it. There was no way I was just going to up and leave my family, kids and all, but the voice of guidance kept coming, stronger, louder, and more persistently. After a year, I couldn't take it anymore, so I gave in and told my then-husband. I explained that I didn't know where this was coming from, or where it was taking me, but that I had to go with it. Breaking up is never easy, but to his credit, he understood that when a change this powerful happens in your life you can't ignore it, so he let me go.

A month or so later, I boarded a plane to Delhi with nothing more than a plan to get a bus to Goa. On my first day there, I met a lady who wanted me to teach her how to tap in to her own guidance and in return offered me food and lodging.

A few weeks later, sitting in the cafe where I'd go to write every day, a man came over and asked what I was working on. I explain it's a book about manifestation, and immediately he asked me to teach him. I started working with him, and in a month he'd manifested the job he really wanted back home in Italy. He gave me the keys to his house and told me to stay as long as I wanted, so I did. I spent a couple months writing, meditating, and trying to understand what was happening to me.

Then my guidance told me I had to meet a teacher called Ramish. I did the research and found him. He was a 102 year old teacher of enlightenment and wisdom known for speaking with deep knowledge of the power of the positive. He taught from his elegant apartment in Mumbai, but it was also common knowledge that he didn't meet with individual students, yet guidance demanded that I meet him alone.

I took the bus to Mumbai and made my way to his apartment in time for one of his lectures. At the end of his talk, he retired to his private room as his team gently ushered all the students out of the large sitting room. I waited until everyone had gone to see if I could meet with him, but of course his people said no. Right then, Ramish popped his head around the door, looked me dead in the eye, and with a smile, asked, "Can you come back at four o'clock?"

"Yes, with pleasure," I replied. For a few hours I wandered around the streets pondering what on earth to say to him, but again guidance cut in: "Tell him that you finally made it and would like to surround him with good intentions and blessings." I almost laughed out loud! How was I meant to give such an enlightened being blessings?

At four I returned to his apartment, where his staff greeted me and showed me into the living room. Ramish appeared with a warm smile and sat opposite me. "You have a message for me?" he asked.

I swallowed in surprise. "Yes, I was told to tell you that I finally made it and that I bring good intentions and blessings to surround you."

"Thank you. I accept your blessings," he said. Then I felt us both enveloped in an extraordinary white light. "Your soul is around us. It is very important that you do not give up on your gift, but your resolve is going to be tested," he said.

We sat in meditation for maybe fifteen minutes, then he got up and asked if he could hug me. As we embraced, I could feel his whole being absolutely radiating love. Gently he let go of me, and said, "Don't worry, your survival will be taken care of." Then he bowed and disappeared back into his room.

After leaving him, guidance took me to Jaipur, as always with no plan or idea why but just forcing me to let go, be in the moment, and trust that I'd be taken care of. I got off the bus and walked through the streets, taking in the city. A local man walked up and introduced himself to me, saying he was an ex-policeman. We talked a little, and hearing of my quest, he invited me to his home. There he introduced me to his grandfather, who took my hands in his and said, "These are healer's hands. You must learn to use them to heal. I will teach you."

I spent an extraordinary month with that wonderful family, working with the grandfather and helping to heal people every day. He taught me that healing is channeling, but more than anything, it's keeping out of the way so that patient and Source can connect for the healing to happen. The healer must put her ego aside and work from a place of love with the grace of humility and the clear intention to serve. Sometimes it's hard not to feel a little pride in it, but pride feeds the ego and clouds the clarity of the healing energy. My time there taught me that we can all be so much more than we think. We are all connected through Spirit, and there really is a healing energy we can all tap into to help bring each other into optimal health.

I left Jaipur profoundly changed and returned to Goa to meet my friend John, who'd come to India on his own spiritual journey. We'd met back home early on in my spiritual unfolding, and I immediately recognized him as a soul mate, or twin flame. We'd planned to do a ten-day silent meditation retreat together months ago, and I hadn't seen him since leaving the states, so it was very special to reconnect with him, and to share that time in the stillness and silence.

Despite the strength of our initial connection, he hadn't been open to a relationship, wanting instead to remain on his spiritual path. During the meditations, his heart opened, and when we finished the retreat, he told me he was ready, he wanted to be with me, and return to America together. Of course, during my ten days of silence, my guides had told me I'm not yet ready for him or a relationship. First I must go to Nepal alone to confront my fear of death. Once again guidance was pulling my life apart, but I knew I had no choice but to follow it. Putting John on the train was such a bittersweet good-bye. I so wanted to be with him, to be taking that journey together, my only solace was in knowing the next time we'd meet, we'd be together forever.

Later that day, I boarded the bus and made the long journey up into the Himalayas. My first night in Kathmandu, I was bitten on the leg by a spider. It swelled quickly, racking my body with fever in just a couple of hours. The hallucinations started the next day with hideous dark entities clawing at my back, scratching evil curses deep into my skin. I was scared and alone in a distant foreign land with no one to help but my guides. They told me a brown recluse spider had bitten me, and it'd kill me if I believed it would. They challenged me to either believe and follow them, or give up and let those dark entities take me. Fighting back the hallucinations, I hung on for dear life, determined not to give in. Logic would say go to a hospital, but lost in the fever's vortex, I didn't know what I believed. After doing the healing work in Jaipur, I'd lost all faith in corporate medicine, and nor did I have the money for it. I knew this was a war within me that I had to win, or I'd die. For almost a week, wave after wave of the hellish fever broke over me as I fell in and out of consciousness, struggling to beat it.

When it finally started to recede, my guides told me to go to Pokhara. I packed up my things and made the twelve-hour journey through the mountains on a bus, throwing up the whole time. I arrived exhausted and dehydrated, and all I could think of was that it's a beautiful place to die. Although the fever abated, my leg looked worse, the bite had grown to the size of half an orange. I checked into a small guesthouse and showed the bite to the owner. He said I had to see a doctor immediately. Taking me by the arm, he led me briskly through the bustling streets to his doctor, who, much to my horror, worked from an open stall in the market. I pulled up my pant leg for him to examine and a gaggle of curious Nepalese gathered round to see what he'd do. He said a brown recluse bit me, and he had to cut open the wound to get the poison out. The thought of having my leg sliced open in a crowd of onlookers with no antiseptic, sterilizers, or pain-killers was more than I could take. I thanked him and left with the small consolation that at least my guides were right about it being a brown recluse bite.

Back in the room, I did my breathing exercises and meditation, but the fever returned. It stole my strength and a paranoia of the darkest kind descended on me. I felt I was dying, all alone, in a foreign country without my children or friends. I passed through the stages of death: anger, denial, frustration, and letting go. Why me? I didn't ask for this. I was happy being a soccer mom in North Carolina. Why did my guidance bring me here to die? I lost all hope, let go and passed out, not expecting to wake up again.

"Get up!" It was them again. At first I ignored them, but they wouldn't let me be. "We told you you'd be taken care of. Now get up!" I was so angry at the voices, these supposed guides, that I wanted to bang my head against the wall just to shut them up, but finally I caved in and did as they said: "Go out into the village."

I pulled myself up off the cot, dressed, and went out into the morning sun. As the crisp mountain air filled my lungs, I knew the worst was behind me.

"Turn right. Go left. Keep walking."

After thirty minutes of their directions, I was hobbling from the pain in my leg. Exhausted, standing in the middle of the street, and surrounded by the snowcapped mountains, I scream, "Please, stop! I can't take this anymore!"

Guidance just shouted back louder. "Keep walking!"

I carried on in such pain that I could barely keep my eyes open. I got to a junction in the road, and looked each way, then exhausted and in agony I asked, "Where now?"

"Look up!" came the reply.

I did, and saw an old man in white robes looking down at me. He was sitting on the wooden platform of a teahouse at the top of a short embankment. His smile glowed with a welcoming **warmth, and** I got the sense he'd been watching me for a while. He beckoned me up to join him, so I clambered up the embankment and sat beside him, broken and exhausted.

"You've lost your faith, haven't you?" he asked gently.

"Yes, but how do you know?" I replied.

"Because I've been waiting here for you for three days."

"What do mean? How did you know I'd be here?"

"The same way you know things," he replied. Then he told me he was a holy man from Kashmir, and the reason he wears white is because he's earned it through years of dedication to his spiritual practice. After spending seven years in absolute silence, he'd become an adept, and was also guided by Spirit. He reignited my faith with his stories, each of which seemed to be a parable to my own journey. As the sun dropped behind the mountain, I asked if I could meet him again tomorrow. He agreed, and tomorrow turned into five days of us meeting.

The wisdom he shared took me through the steps of my death. One day at a time, I experienced anger, denial, frustration, grief, and acceptance, but not just through his words. He made each lesson an experience that illustrated the point he was making: walking barefoot on a mountain path, swimming in the ice-cold water, going hungry and thirsty, and pushing my physical limits at the same time as expanding my understanding. Then at the end of the fifth day, he said he's done what he came here to do. It was time for him to return to Kashmir and me to America.

As we hugged and said good-bye, he also told me to take the poison out of my leg before making the journey back to Delhi. I returned to the lodge, where I borrowed a sharp knife from another traveler, went to my room, and pulled myself together. I got into the shower and turned on the cold water to keep myself present before asking my guides to help. They appeared before me, guiding my hand, showing me how to cut open the bite and push the poisons out. I removed the center of the infection, which was about the size of a half-dollar. It was so painful that I almost passed out, but I keep pouring on the alcohol and bandaged it tight to keep out the fire ants. In my delirium, I'd imagined them crawling into the open wound and building a nest!

Slowly, the pain subsided, and I was soon able to return to my meditation and writing. I wrote for days until my leg healed.

AM: *So did you get back to your friend John?*

Hope: He returned to Charlotte, but once I get back to the States, my guides wanted me to go to New York to get my book published. While I was there, he died in a freak accident. His death tore my heart out and made me want to throw all this away, none of it made sense anymore. I descend into a deep, dark place for a long time. Then one day, as my guides were coming through, I noticed a different energy, a new voice. It was John, he'd come back as my guide and my teacher. I've learnt so much from him, including that our destiny is to be together, just not in the way I'd thought. I wanted it to be an emotional, earthly bond, but of course that's not what the fates had in store.

Now I really understand that death isn't the end, it's just a change. We are all inseparable because we really are all one. It isn't an easy path following your guides, putting your life in their hands, and doing what they suggest. I still struggle with the challenges of it. Here in the South, people get scared of Spirit. They think it's a threat to their beliefs, but they're so wrapped up in a prepackaged projection of God that they'll never experience what God is.

AM: *Following the voice of guidance takes tremendous courage, as does sharing your story so openly. Thank you, Hope.*

Section Two

The Panel of Experts

Chapter 16

The Seers

Seeking to understand my own experiences, I'd spoken to many so-called psychics in the past, but very little of what any of them said either rang true **or** happened, so I came into this with an unusual mix of skepticism and experience.

However to help understand the stories you've just read, I needed to find a group of bonafide mediums with a real communion to the other side. Some came through those stories, the others came through friends, recommendations and research. Many are published and have been on TV, both in their own shows and as special guests on others. I read their books if they were published, and had readings with all of them to be certain they were for real. Everyone here passed the acid test: naming and describing my closest deceased family members with absolute accuracy and giving me messages of things that nobody could possibly know.

In this section I introduce our panel of experts by asking how their experiences with Spirit begun and what their process of working with it is, to give a sense of who they are and how they work. Then, in the following section of the book, I ask them all the same ten questions of Spirit to see if through their answers, we can glimpse a unified insight into the mysteries of what lies beyond. Finally in the sixth section of the book I return to them to ask their advice for both parents and children in dealing with the gift of being able to communicate through the veil.

Chapter 17

Carissa Schumacher

I was introduced to Carissa Schumacher through Scott Nathan and his remarkable story of finding his birth father through her. After conducting our interviews, she invited me to join her for one of the Spirit retreats she organizes in Sedona, Arizona. It was an incredible experience that allowed me to see firsthand the healing and transformative power of her gift of reconnecting people to loved ones.

AM: *When did this begin for you?*

Carissa: When I was very young, I remembered fragments of past lives, memories of the time before the womb, and even selecting my parents. I remember the moment I entered the womb through a tunnel of radiant, almost ultraviolet light. It's exactly the same tunnel I've seen during several near-death experiences. The similarities between these two experiences helped me realize that we're constantly rebirthed from one life to the next in the soul's journey of evolution.

I was born with a rare form of synesthesia called electromagnetic synesthesia. It enables me to sense, see, and hear light and sound frequencies that are normally undetectable. When I close my eyes, even in total sensory deprivation, I see an entire world of colors, visions, vibrations, and energies. These are always present around all of us, and my sense of this extrasensory perception is that it's innate within us all, just as bats and dolphins "see" with sonar, birds navigate using the earth's electromagnetic field, and dogs can track scents for miles. I thought everyone experienced the world this way as a child,. My parents thought nothing of my invisible friends, or perhaps just accepted it as the vivid imagination of a child. By five, I was spending long periods of time meditating in nature. I used to take offerings to Mother Earth in little "God boxes" that I made and buried all over our property to please the Spirit energies that constantly appeared to me.

I grew up in the Revolutionary War town of Westport, Connecticut, where every night before bed I heard the sound of marching and felt the presence of young soldiers. It was there by a stream, that I encountered my first spirit guide, a powerful Mohawk Iroquois warrior who's remained with me ever since. It's also where I learned how to help spirits trapped in this dimension, cross over to the next. I'd see them coming towards me as wispy energies first, then as they got close they'd take form. Sometimes they'd reveal a word, name, or message; other times they'd be silent. As they neared my heart space, they'd turn around, as though backing into me while taking a last look at the world, and then they'd dissolve through a gateway in my heart. Sometimes I'd feel the pain they carried in life, but as they crossed over, all their pain transmuted and dissolved into love.

Although this was spontaneous and natural, it troubled me tremendously as a child. After these Spirit encounters I used to get terrible asthma attacks, so I tried to turn off my ability. Many years later a shamanic elder described it to me as crossing Spirit into the light by serving as a human portal that the Lakota shamans and the adepts of the ancient Mayan and Egyptian civilizations all did.

I never spoke about any of this with the kids at school because I just wanted to be normal and fit in, but one day we went on a field trip to a historic cemetery. It was the first time I'd been to one, and the moment we arrived I was overwhelmed with anxiety and fear. Everywhere I looked, energies were pulling at me. I couldn't close my eyes because I'd see and hear them even more intensely, tugging at me from under the earth. It was so real and so traumatic that I became hysterical. My teacher carried me back to the bus where I sat sobbing on my own for hours. That's when I decided to try and push it all away, to close myself off from it, but of course I couldn't. Spirit was always there. I started living a double life, at school I'd study and try to be a normal kid, then in the evening I'd commune with Spirit. My sensitivities made it hard for me to be in crowds for long, too, so I'd never go to concerts or clubs, which added to my isolation.

After high school, I went to Brown and got my degree studying neuroscience and psychic phenomena. There I discovered that science is corroborating the basis for intuitive and empathic abilities and that many new theories in physics and neuroscience are in sync with the teachings of the ancients. For example, the Aboriginal creation story depicts the world as being composed of a web of interconnected strings or vibrations called songlines, an idea that is quite similar to the concept of string theory.

AM: *So when did you start to share your gift again?*

Carissa: Not till I was at college. I did my first readings and energy channelings there, but after I left I tried to fit into the corporate world and suppressed my gift again. I soon realized that world wasn't for me. No matter how hard you try, you can't escape your true self, so I left the nine-to-five world behind and began studying with a series of shamans and monks. That's when I realized my higher purpose is to serve by connecting people to Spirit and their own divine selves through our work together.

AM: *What is your process, and how do you experience Spirit?*

Carissa: I place myself in a position of calm receivership, clear my mind, then put myself in a deep meditative space within my womb and heart. That tunes me to the right channel for each reading. Like with a radio, there are countless channels carrying all sorts of different frequencies and vibrations. For example, tuning into a higher-frequency entity like an angel or spirit guide who has not physically incarnated, you find a completely different quality of energy than that of a recently deceased spirit.

I don't just connect the living to the passed. I also help to connect people to their higher selves so they can master their karmic lessons, illuminate their higher purpose, and find a deeper peace and harmony in their lives. Reconnecting with Source, the ability to commune with the divine resides within all of us. When you make the conscious choice to step onto that path, choosing to enlighten above all else, you rediscover and reclaim your relationship to Spirit. When you commit to Source, Source commits to you.

AM: *How has your work with Spirit influenced your personal view of religion?*

Carissa: The concept of religion baffles me. Everything is energy and vibration, so everything has to be Spirit, and it's all made of the fabric of the divine. We're all equal in our divinity and humanity, we're all one, but the world's religions breed separation. They all say there is only one way to be whole or righteous, and that is to subscribe to their belief system. If we don't, we're an infidel, a heretic, or pariah, and we're cast out for our transgression. This primitive, tribalistic separation goes against the very principle of Spirit. Anything that separates us or judges us, goes against the essence of unconditional love that the great teachers such as Christ and Buddha spoke of.

Christ didn't pick up a crossbow and start killing his enemies, nor did Gandhi pull out a gun when stones were being thrown at him. Any man who has spilt another man's blood in the name of God must question what that means. If your God wants you to kill, that God will also want someone else to kill you, your family, and your friends. Does that really sound like the will of the Creator, or a God you want to follow?

Spirituality and religion should inform each other. Your religion can augment or guide your spirituality, but it doesn't have to define it. If humanity woke up to the freedom of their divine Spirit, we'd lose our fear of judgment, and the walls of separation instilled in us by those archaic, socioreligious power structures would evaporate. However, that doesn't mean renouncing religion altogether, but questioning what parts of a belief system truly resonate with you. Let go of what you've been conditioned to believe in, and just take the teachings that inspire you. No one can tell you how to experience your relationship with the divine because the divine is unique and different for each and every one of us. Learn to commune with the divine, with Spirit, through meditation and contemplation. Spiritual freedom is seeking your own path and discovering the joy of illuminating the divine within yourself. Be in compassion, patience, and love, towards yourself and everyone else. That way, you'll live your life on the path of light, regardless of whether you are religious.

AM: *What a wonderful insight. Thank you.*

Chapter 18

Hollister Rand

I first heard of Hollister Rand through Dawn Baillie. When I asked her if she'd be in the book she invited me to one of her Spirit demonstrations here in Los Angeles. It was held in a small meeting hall, which was full to the brim with around 120 people, and the messages that came through for forty or more of them were all spot on. A mother whose daughter had just committed suicide reduced the room to tears as her daughter, through Hollister, asked that her ashes be scattered with the whales and dolphins. Sobbing, the mother said that's what she'd been considering, but she didn't know if that's what her daughter wanted. Hearing her get the answer directly from the other side was one of the many stunning, heartbreaking, and beautiful moments of that four-hour session. It gave me the feeling of connection to Spirit that no church or synagogue has ever done, and I left finally understanding why Spirit identified itself to Moses as simply "I am that I am."

To find out more about Hollister visit her website: www.hollisterrand.com. I can also highly recommend her book *I'm Not Dead, I'm Different*. It's a great and insightful must-read from one of the most powerful mediums I've come across.

AM: *Hollister, when did your experience with Spirit begin?*

Hollister: When I was very young. They showed up all the time, out in the garden, in the house, on the stairs, even in my bedroom. I didn't think of them as spirits, they were just other kinds of people who were also in my life. I didn't understand what Spirit meant until my grandfather passed away and then appeared to me. That's when it really clicked. It wasn't till I started school, and talking to the other kids, that I realized most people don't see the spirits.

AM: *What is your process and how do you experience Spirit?*

Hollister: My process has changed from when I first started seeing and communicating with spirits. As I said, I could hardly tell the difference between a spirit and a person as a kid, but now that I've been doing this work for many years, the spirits have changed how they communicate with me. Mainly I still see them, either standing there in front of me as they were in life (objective clairvoyance) or by them showing me images in my mind's eye (subjective clairvoyance). They'll often highlight a part of themselves that's very identifiable to the person I'm reading for. Instead of seeing an entire person in front of me, a spirit will show me the color of his eyes, hands, a tooth pattern, or a hairstyle he was known for.

They've gotten good at using all of my other senses to get messages across. I get sounds, feelings, thoughts, and smells. I've become very good at recognizing perfumes, or if someone smoked pot a lot, I'll smell pot. I get tastes, too—favorite things they liked to eat. I'm also clairaudient, which means I hear Spirit. Sometimes they'll speak and give me their names. I'll hear it inside my head (subjective clairaudience) like I'm wearing headphones, and sometimes I'll hear it outside my head (objective clairaudience) just like someone's speaking into my ear. They'll highlight identifiers, the things that let them be instantly recognized, and then they'll fill in the details through my clairsentience, my feeling for how they were, how they passed, or what their personality was like.

AM: *How has this influenced your opinion of religion?*

Hollister: Being a medium, it's my job to make my talents available to both the spirits and the people who come to me. I find it's best not to have any judgment about any particular religion. I've had people from all the major religions come to me, and I've even had spirits argue among themselves in a session about God. One was an atheist, the other a Catholic, and they were arguing about it in the afterlife. The lady who came to see me said it was her father and father-in-law, who used to have that argument at the family's Christmas dinner every year. Honestly, I'm still not sure whether I was being shown that the argument is still continuing because there's no answer to it or if they were just using the argument as an identifier. Either way, she had no doubt that's who came through because that's exactly what they always did together.

Another lady who came to me from the afterlife during a session said, "I wanted to die to see the face of God." Her daughter told me those were her last words. Of course I had to ask her if she saw the face of God, but she replied that she didn't because God is everywhere and everything. I'd say God is uncontainable, far greater than any religion, and maybe, like what the universe is expanding into, God is far beyond anything we can understand. Sometimes in readings I get certain expressions of it, but I'm leaving the question of the nature of God entirely open. I'll take what the spirits give me in the framework of their own understanding and the understanding of those they left behind. If a kid's spirit says, "Mom, I made it to heaven," I say it exactly as I heard it, without any embellishment as to what that heaven might be like. They know between themselves what their belief is. It is not my job to overlay my belief on top of theirs.

Chapter 19

THOMAS JOHN

I met Thomas John through a friend in Los Angeles who was absolutely insistent I include him in the book and arranged for me to meet with him while he was in town from New York. He did a quick reading that hit so many spot-on points so quickly that it left no doubt in my mind that he's the real deal. You can see more of who he is and what he does on his website: www.mediumthomas.com.

AM: *Thomas, when did this begin for you?*

Thomas: As far back as I can remember, I'd see things and presences around people. I'd see things in dreams, too, but I always thought it was normal and that everybody experienced it. As I got older, it got a lot stronger, and of course I realized that not everyone has this ability.

AM: *Did it separate you from the other kids at school?*

Thomas: It started to be a bit of a problem when I was nine or ten because I'd talk to 'people' the other kids couldn't see, so that made me seem weird and as a result I spent a lot of time on my own. That's when my parents really realized I was different, too.

AM: *What is your process? How do you experience Spirit?*

Thomas: I am primarily claircognizant, but I use the full spectrum of 'clairs'. Most commonly I'd say I use clairaudience, clairsentience, and clairvoyance. If I'm going to do a reading, I put myself in that mind-set and usually just meditate. I'll start with a protection prayer and ask for whatever's supposed to come through to come through, and then I'll just sit in silence for a couple of moments. That clears my mind and opens me up to read the person I'm about to work with. When I sit with people, I just start knowing things, it's almost like I get their memories or thoughts. When something does come through, it's pretty clear, and if I can't pick anything up, I ask Spirit to show me. If something then reiterates itself over and over, I start to explain it and describe it to the person. That's the core of how I work, but I also see images, hear words, or pick up on smells, and sometimes it all comes at once.

AM: *How has your work with Spirit influenced your personal view of religion?*

Thomas: I was raised Catholic, but I don't spend a lot of time thinking about religion. It's a concept I don't really connect with, as it causes so many problems. It splits people apart when its goal should be to unify, so honestly, it's really never resonated with me. I have spent some time reading the Bible, trying to understand what it says about what I do, but honestly, I feel it's cloaked in superstition and entirely misses the point. What I do almost helps validate it because I'm showing direct evidence that there is something beyond. Doing the thousands and thousands of readings I've done, and hopefully will continue to do, the spirits always talk about what it's like over there. I've had serial killers, terrorists, and people who've had horrible problems in life come through, and they've never described a hell or spoken about being punished. Honestly, I believe that religion's dogma of a heaven and hell is just a misconception. The spirits do often speak of an organizing principle over there, which has led me to believe that there's something beyond this physical plane that does in some way control things. I believe it's a presence that resides within us and outside of us, and I often recognize it doing the work. But there's really not a word that describes it, except maybe love.

Chapter 20

LISA WILLIAMS

Lisa Williams is originally from the United Kingdom, but on a trip to LA she met the famous TV producer Merv Griffin by happenstance. He was so impressed with her powers that he created two TV series for her. She's also appeared on *Oprah*, *Jimmy Kimmel*, and *Larry King*, to name a few, and is a published author. Her book *The Survival of the Soul* is incredibly illuminating and inspiring, and it's an absolute must-read for anyone interested in the subject. To find out more about Lisa check out her website: www.lisawilliams.com.

Lisa also runs the website Kids with Gifts, which is packed with information for kids who discover they have the ability and want to know more: kidswithgifts.squarespace.com.

AM: *When did your experience with Spirit begin?*

Lisa: When I was very young, maybe three or four years old. I was always seeing spirits and hearing people talking to me.

AM: *How do you experience Spirit?*

Lisa: In so many ways! If I'm doing a reading, I sit down and do a meditation to clear the space around me. This allows me to open up. I ask for protection and for the best form of communication possible, and then I ask Spirit to come forward and share the information that's relevant for my client. As Spirit draws close to me, I can feel its energy entering my aura. Then I start seeing things, the person may appear in front of me, or sometimes, I'll be shown visions in my mind's eye. That's how they come in or introduce themselves. Then I'll start hearing them. That's how I work the most in session, by hearing them. I open up my senses and allow the information to flow, but you can't just be passive, you have to engage them all the time, like you're interviewing them. Always asking more questions.

AM: *How has your work with Spirit influenced your personal view of religion?*

Lisa: As a kid, I wanted to be a nun. I was in the Church of England school and knew I had this calling, so I thought it was a religious thing and that it should be my path. The school was very churchy, we'd always be going to assembly, singing hymns, and praying. Oddly enough, even though I grew up in that headspace, my father was an atheist and didn't believe in God at all. Through the church I learned that a religious person is not necessarily spiritual, and of course, that a spiritual person is not necessarily religious. I do believe there's something there, no matter what you call it. God, the Divine, the Force, the Source, it's all one and the same, and like it or not, we're all a part of it. Overall, I think that as long as you have belief, you should believe in yourself, because you are a part of the divine.

AM: *What a lovely way of putting it, thank you.*

Chapter 21

Jeffrey Wands

I met Jeffrey Wands though Valerie Jean Garduno and immediately warmed to him. The first time we spoke, he described my father in his Royal Air Force uniform and gave me a message that only my dad would say. Between our initial conversation, which was randomly scheduled for December 21, 2012, the day the world was due to end, and doing his interview, I had a chance to read his books: *The Psychic In You*, *Another Door Opens*, and *Knock and the Door Will Open.* I can recommend them all. They're packed full of great stories and excellent information. Jeffrey lives in New York, where he is regularly on WALK 97.5-FM and does many other local events. Learn more about Jeffrey by visiting his website: www.jeffreywands.com.

AM: *When did your experience with Spirit begin?*

Jeffrey: It started when I was maybe five or six. One day when I was in trouble my great-grandmother, Mary, whom I never met. She appeared to me saying my mom shouldn't be punishing me because she was way worse when she was a kid. Initially my mom didn't believe it, but then Mary told me how Granddad would come home drunk on his old horse and gave me its name along with a bunch of other things I'd never have known.

AM: *What's your process? How do you experience Spirit?*

Jeffrey: It comes in different ways. Sometimes I feel them, or I hear them, or they touch me. Usually, it starts with hearing them. I'll pick up a change of energy, like a low frequency buzzing or low voices chattering. Then I'll get people or figures and symbolism. It's different with every person and situation, and rarely the same twice.

AM: *How has your work with Spirit affected your view on religion?*

Jeffrey: It's important to have religion because Spirit likes prayer and the music of prayers. It doesn't matter what the religion is, it's about having faith and knowing there is a higher power. I've read for people of all faiths, and their concerns are as universal as the messages of love that come from the other side. I do get frustrated when religion is used by people to judge others, or these gifts, just because they don't understand it. I've been attacked on national TV by people who assume their belief is the only way and say this work is wrong because it says so in the Bible. I see religion used as a crutch for ignorance, narrow-mindedness, and stupidity more than I see it used as a guidebook for loving, accepting, and honoring a spiritual path, which is what it really should be.

Chapter 22

California Psychics: Demi, Eden, and James

In every business, there's an 800-pound gorilla, and in the world of communing with Spirit, it doesn't get any bigger than California Psychics. With a million visits to the company's website every week, over a million customers who've had one-on-one phone readings, 24/7 service, and an almost unimaginable level of customer engagement, California Psychics is one of the most trusted names in the field.

People call California Psychics for a vast range of reasons: love, career, self-discovery, a new perspective on their life path, and of course, to reach out to those no longer here. To become one of its psychics requires passing some very stringent tests. On average, only two out of every hundred applicants are chosen to join the team, and once they're on board, the level of customer feedback is instant, so only those who really make the grade survive. The company currently has well over three hundred carefully screened and selected mediums across United States, Canada, and the United Kingdom, so I asked the team there if they would pick three of their top-tier mediums to join our panel of experts. They connected me with their readers Demi, Eden, and James. The company's privacy policy requires that they work using pseudonyms; hence, they're the only people in the book not using their full names.

Demi

AM: *When did your experience with Spirit begin?*

Demi: Very early on. Honestly, this has always been my reality. I remember when I was two or three, the only way I could tell the difference between who was here and who wasn't, was to go up and touch them. I'd always be touching people to make sure they were real. Sometimes I'd get spirits from different time periods, which I could tell by their clothing, but the spirits were always crystal clear, not hazy.

AM: *How did your parents deal with it?*

Demi: They were very supportive, but it runs in my family. My grandmother channels, my great grandmother channels, and so does my granddad on the opposite side. Six years before I was born, my parents were told I was coming and that I'd be born with "the veil," which in our culture is an indication of intuitive ability. They were also told I'd have blond hair and blue eyes, which is very unusual in my Hispanic family, so as soon as they saw me, they knew.

AM: *How do you experience Spirit?*

Demi: Constantly! All day long, in sleep and awake, every moment of my day has aspects of it, it's a constant download. It's a running joke at home because I'm always getting information. I'm just a conduit, a speaker box. I get the information and I just voice what I hear. I'll be talking to children, and suddenly, I'll get the video screen in my mind's eye of something that's going to happen. Sometimes it's a silly thing that'll happen an hour later, but with global events like natural disasters, it usually comes a couple of days beforehand. As a kid I used to draw these events down, and they'd always happen just as I'd drawn them.

AM: *How has your work with Spirit influenced your personal view of religion?*

Demi: I've studied quite a bit of theology, and I don't have an opinion that one is right and one is wrong. On a global level, the core of every religion leads to the same thing. They're all looking for a way to connect to the divine, the Source. Sure, history, language, and culture will change the stories or color their idea of the Source, but all the prophets have come from the same place. What we need is an understanding that we're all from the same place, and that's why I encompass all the faiths and work with anyone who is pure of heart.

Eden

AM: *When did your experience with Spirit begin for you?*

Eden: Around seven, when I came down with a very bad case of the measles. I had a high fever for several days and was delirious. During that time, an older female came to me in my mind's eye and told me I'd be getting well soon. After about twenty hours, my fever broke, and I got well. I told my mother about the vision, describing the woman and what she was wearing. My mother immediately recognized her as my great-grandmother. That was the first time she came to me, but throughout my life she's come to tell me I'm going to get better during any health crisis. I also had dreams about people in the neighborhood when they made their transition. I'd tell my mother when I got up, and she'd tell me they passed away in the night.

AM: *What is your process? How do you experience Spirit?*

Eden: Depends, but mostly mine comes through clairvoyance and clairaudience. I'll see pictures in my head, and then I hear voices. In the beginning, I had to learn how to distinguish it because I thought it was all my own voice, but as time went on I learned to distinguish between the voices. I'm very clear about making boundaries, so I haven't ever had a physical manifestation in front of me, as I've asked not to. I'll hear things and feel things, and then information comes through as a knowing. It's not a guessing game, it's very pronounced. You just know it, and there's no reason to question it. The most important thing is to push ego aside. It doesn't matter if things don't make sense to you, just relay the information as you get it. Talking to spirits who've passed over is not something you do for your personal benefit. You're just a messenger, it's not your job to understand, the message isn't for you, it's for your client.

AM: *How has your work with Spirit influenced your personal view of religion?*

Eden: I was raised a strict Roman Catholic and was brought up to believe it was the only true religion, but what I've found is that true religion is not anywhere out there. It's inside of you. It's a seed that opens up and reveals itself, a personal thing. As I grew up, I realized that all religions are man-made. They're all just stories and legends filtered through the human mind, subject to the social biases of their cultures. The only real connection is your personal connection to your creator, to what you believe.

When I was diagnosed with terminal cancer two years ago, I had the best doctors you can have, but they told me I had two months to live. The knowing inside me said, "That's not so. You're going to beat this." I listened to that voice and told my doctors: "No one can tell me when I'm going to die. That's between me and my God." Well, here I am two years later, cancer free.

I'll take things I like from different religions. I understand the rights and rituals of Catholicism from a new perspective. Psychic mediumship has allowed me to understand things I never would have conceptualized with my rational mind. I was doing a reading two years ago for a lady with her deceased sister. Well, I kept seeing a young man wearing glasses and was able to describe him in detail. The deceased sister then told me to ask her living sister about the abortion. I did, and she replied that her sister had indeed had an abortion eighteen years ago. Well, that aborted child still grew up, but in a different dimension, the dimension of Spirit, and was now with the deceased sister. That was a revelation for me, and I now realize that even an unborn child who doesn't have an existence here still continues to grow and live in Spirit.

I've read that the human eye only sees about 10 percent of what's really around us. Spirit isn't in a far-off galaxy. It's right here, right now. It's just we aren't sensitized to it. Doing this work, I've learned that life absolutely continues after death, and we are so much more than our human experience. I'm extremely grateful for being able to do this work and for the understanding it has given me.

James

AM: *When did your experience with Spirit begin?*

James: Back in 1997. Walking past a local guitar shop here in England, an acoustic guitar caught my eye, and on the spur of the moment, I went in and bought it. The first piece of music I taught myself was John Denver's *Leaving on a Jet Plane* because I really connected with the song. I bought a lot more of his music, but then he died in that plane crash. It affected me deeply, as did his songs of the beauty of America, and I really got into the idea of the Old West.

My wife then bought me a book about Native Americans, and in it there was a picture of a Dakota Sioux called Long Wolf that really grabbed my attention. I started reading his story, and it turns out he toured England with Buffalo Bill Cody's *Wild West* show, but died of pneumonia while he was in London. His wife had him buried in Brompton Cemetery because she was afraid she'd never be able to transport his body all the way back home. Reading this I was overcome with the desire to get him back to his home, so I called the cemetery to ask where his grave was only to discover that his body had been returned to Pine Ridge Reservation in South Dakota the previous week.

After that I started becoming more aware of my feelings, intuitions, and my heart's desire to be in nature. Inspiring and guiding messages started coming through, and the calling grew louder and louder. I followed as my instincts lead me to a weeklong Native American drumming course at a beautiful old house deep in the English countryside. There were over three hundred people there, and the vibe was great, but I didn't really know why I was there until one evening I heard a single drum being played down near the lake. Even though it was just a single drum, it was so full of emotion, energy, and power that I was drawn to it. Walking toward the lake, I noticed a woman twenty or so years my senior also being drawn to it. We went down to the lake and sat in silence with the drummer. I closed my eyes, and the rhythm took me into a vision. I was transported to a place I've never seen where something terrible had happened. There was snow on the ground, and the people around me were all Native Americans. Everyone was crying, huddled over dead loved ones or holding their heads in their hands. There were bodies and death everywhere, but even though the living were in a terrible state of sadness and disarray, as I walked through the remnants of the camp I was overwhelmed by the strength of their love.

The drumming stopped and I came back into my body. Opening my eyes I watched the solitary drummer stand and walk away. Then the older lady and I stood up, nodded at each other, and went our separate ways. I never saw that lone drummer again, but later that day the lady waved me over in the dining hall, saying she needed to talk with me in private. We found a quiet spot, sat down together, and she looked me right in the eye and said, "You were where I was, you were at Wounded Knee, weren't you?"

I hadn't heard the name before, but I described my vision to her. She nodded and said, "That's it, and that's the drum beat they played at Wounded Knee the day after the massacre." That's how it really started for me, and I'm very grateful for my awakening.

AM: *What is your process? How do you experience Spirit?*

James: After my awakening, I'd go to local spiritualist churches to learn and study. The mediums would always come to me saying I should be up there with them. I'd politely refuse, but they'd keep coming and coming. Then an older lady visited our local church, took one look at me, and said, "You will come to me once a week, and I will teach you."

Over the next eight months, I did, and she taught me how to breathe and get my ego out of the way to allow Spirit to come through. From the discipline of her training, I can now sit for about three minutes, quiet myself within, and say a prayer of preparation, usually the Lord's Prayer, before working. Clairsentience is my main source of connection. I feel the sorrow and grief whether on the phone or in person, and I feel the love, too, Spirit love. There is nothing like it in this world. It's completely humbling and overwhelming when it comes through. It is so profound and powerful that I'll often be sobbing like a baby when it touches me.

AM: *How has your work with Spirit influenced your personal view of religion?*

James: I've never been that religious, and honestly, I feel its message has gotten very messed up over time. I used to be a postman, walking around the local villages delivering mail. Everyone knew me. They'd smile and wave, but when I told the church folk I was working with Spirit, they completely shunned me, saying I was doing the devil's work.

I believe that I'm a creation of the divine Source and inseparable from it. There is one source of all creation, everything is part of it and connected to it. We cannot separate ourselves from it. Since we are all one, we should not be split apart by the notions of any religion.

Chapter 23

Antony Galvan

Lastly, I wanted to introduce a wild card, a modern-day spiritual searcher with a fascinating take on healing and Spirit. Primarily, Antony Galvan is a sound healer, but what interested me are his journeys as a searcher, seeker, and experimental thinker. He's lived and trained with the shaman elders from the Seicoia tribe of the Ecuadorian Amazon, where his experience with Spirit comes from a people who live in harmony with nature, something long lost to those of us in the industrialized world.

AM: *How did your work in the realm of Spirit begin?*

Antony: I had a few profound experiences in my early adulthood that freed me from the shackles of this identity, the person, and my ego. I realized then, that I was vastly more than I thought or had been taught, I was a tiny part of everything I'd been told God was, and was totally inseparable from it. A genuine primary experience of such power and clarity makes it impossible not to proceed down a spiritual path in your life.

AM: *So how did that influence your view of religion?*

Antony: Ultimately, religion fails us because it doesn't speak to the primary part of the mind that experiences things. All the religions have people gather in buildings to listen to someone read from a book about someone else's primary experience in the past, and agree on it. That's vastly different from having your own primary experience, your own burning bush, your own time sitting under the Bodhi Tree, or wandering in the desert. Religion seeks to follow in the footsteps of the wise, where spirituality pushes you to uncover your own wisdom through experience. We need to respect that everyone's sacred path is his own and encourage him to walk it while expanding his spiritual horizons with support and guidance.

AM: *That sounds like the old Pythagorean idea of not writing teachings down because it removes them from the present, and true wisdom can only be taught by experiencing it in the present.*

Antony: Yes, the wisdom schools of ancient Egypt and Greece used techniques for people to have individual experiences. Growth happens when an unknown, becomes a known and turns into knowledge. While all religions would have you learn from their teachings what is already known. In essence, that is stagnancy. Learning, the lust for growth, is innate in us all. We are all God, and God is us, we just need to wake up to that.

AM: *In your quest to learn, you've studied with many shamans and teachers. How has that informed your current beliefs?*

Antony: Once you enter the jungle, you're immersed in a civilization whose culture is completely rooted in nature. They are really at one with their environment and hold it in such high esteem that I could only liken it to a mixture of deepest awe and love. The art of the Seicoia tribe is based on the visions of the ayahuasca ceremonies. Ayahuasca is a plant-based cocktail, not unlike peyote, that connects you to the heartbeat of all creation and is taken in a very specific religious ritual. Their entire culture is immersed in it, it's a part of the fabric of who they are, their belief system, their cultural mores, everything. Seeing the difference between their unbroken, multi-millennial spiritual practice and our frantically paced eclectic culture affected me deeply.

In the West, we're all mixed and matched, a salad of different aspects of other cultures, and all of them are based in the past. Our religion comes from one place, our yoga or martial arts from another, and our nutritional ideas from another. The Seicoia culture is an unwavering, undiluted purity of dedication to a single, traditional spiritual path that is based on the individual's experience in the present.

AM: *Would you describe yourself as a shaman?*

Antony: I'm a sound healer and a guide, but I'd never call myself a shaman. I've been with real shamans. They're like the Dalai Lama, recognized at birth, other worldly creations, special beings. I'm just a guide with a deep insight into things that are currently considered on the fringe, but people are starting to get into a desire to explore their own psychology. To quote Terence McKenna's often used metaphor, "Psychedelics are to psychology what telescopes are to astronomy." You can wax poetic about Kierkegaard and Hegel, Kant, Freud, or Jung, but all of their wonderful pontifications go out the window with one ayahuasca experience.

There's a documentary on YouTube called *Stepping into the Fire* that has really brought the idea of psychedelic exploration back in the lexicon. In the sixties, we had wild-card spokespeople like Timothy Leary, but now we have doctors, scientists, chemists, and people in the health industry talking about it. You can have a truly mystical experience, a glimpse of something so much more vast and so startlingly vibrant and real that you can't help but be impacted when you return to reality. It absolutely changes people's lives.

AM: *Thank you, those are great insights.*

Section Three

The Questions for Spirit

Chapter 24

Curiosity

Now that you've met our experts, whom I consider to be a gold-standard group with real contact to Spirit, it's time to get to the core of this project: my quest to understand what and where Spirit is. However, before we do, I'd like to share one more personal story:

A few years ago on my usual dawn hike with the pups, I got the sense of someone right behind me. I spun around, but there wasn't anybody there. I carried on walking, but the sense of a presence kept getting stronger, so I said out loud, "I can feel you're here. If you want to walk with me, please do, and if you have a message for me, I'm open to receive it." In that moment I suddenly felt a thousand people walking in step with me, stretched away off each shoulder. Instinctively, I knew it was the Macpherson side of my family, with its thousand-year history. Then inside my head, just as if I were wearing headphones, I heard the same two lines of the 23rd Psalm my father said at my mother's funeral, and knew I was being given a life lesson at the deepest soul level:

"Yea, though I walk through the valley of the shadow of death..."

This is the journey through life, because nobody gets out of here alive.

"I will fear no evil: for thou art with me; thy rod and thy staff they comfort me."

Have no fear because I'm here with you, and I'm protecting you.

I was deeply touched, but despite the incredible emotional impact of the moment, I was also rather puzzled. My father was in great health over in London, so I didn't really understand what the message and the visitation meant. I completed the hike, then ten minutes after I got home, the phone rang. It was my brother calling from London with the news that my father had died of a sudden and unexpected heart attack forty-five minutes ago, exactly when I was at the top of the hill.

A Second World War pilot, race-car driver, and self-confessed agnostic, he lived an octane-rich life in the fast lane. He wasn't someone to talk about spirits, ghosts, or anything in the least bit philosophical, yet in the interviews I did with our mediums he kept appearing in his RAF uniform and giving me messages that could have come from no one but him.

As you can see, my own experiences have convinced me that Spirit is real. The love, hope, and evidence in its messages prove its extraordinary insight into our lives, so I asked our mediums the same ten questions in this section of the book in the hope of glimpsing a new understanding of Spirit's perspective of this reality,

Chapter 25

How is Spirit Bound to Matter?

Our physical bodies are matter, stardust, a part of this incredible universe of creation, and decay, but we are also Spirit. My first question attempts to discover what it is that binds our eternal Spirit to this mortal coil, our material body, giving us this extraordinary experience of life.

AM: *How is Spirit bound to matter?*

Hollister Rand: This physical realm of matter is a container for Spirit. Our own bodies are a vehicle to allow the all-creative to experience creation, giving Spirit communion with the physical realm and all its inherent limits like time and gravity.

Lisa Williams: It's my understanding that we're all souls encapsulated in this vessel we call a body. We have to learn to treasure our bodies as our temples of life. It's vital that we love, respect, and accept them for what they are, regardless of size or shape. Our souls are attached to our bodies by a silver cord that is our life force, like an umbilical cord connecting mother and baby. It's connected at our solar plexus, which is why you often get a gut reaction. It's your soul letting you know something's wrong, it's saying, "No, no, no!" And your body feels it at that point of connection. When we astral travel, or leave our bodies in near-death experiences, it's this elastic silver cord that keeps us connected, and when it's severed is when we depart, or die.

Jeffrey Wands: Spirit is beyond matter. It is the purest energy. Matter can't be created or destroyed, but it can be altered by energy. In my experience, Spirit contains the soul and the soul's memories. Making the connection to Spirit always brings out a specific soul's past, reflecting Spirit's ability to take on many different forms.

Demi of California Psychics: Spirit is bound to matter by the divine spark. I have a science background and figured this out doing gross anatomy and dissection. The difference between a cadaver and a human being is that divine spark, a light that radiates out from the core into the auric body. You can see it in every living thing. As long as you're breathing, you can tap into it. Some people absolutely radiate it, it fills up the room when they walk in, but others have just a little flicker. My job is making theirs burn brighter by bringing it into the divine love.

Eden of California Psychics: I am being told it's the breath of God.

James of California Psychics: I can feel it, but I can't describe it beyond saying it's by love from the Source, the highest energy flow of Spirit working with absolutely pure, unconditional love. It doesn't judge what we should be, wanting nothing more than for us to experience it. We aren't yet able to fully attune to it in its entirety because we're still such imperfect creatures.

Antony Galvan: Based on my own experience, I'd say by a core essence of vibrations. Sinusoidal studies are now revealing the effects of sound on matter, so I'd say it's the primal sound, the word of God, the 'Om'. I see everything as a giant song, a symphony of Spirit.

Thomas John: Spirit coming into matter is a manifestation of the Great Spirit, but it's not a permanent bond. It's only something that can be maintained for a brief period of time, which is why everything dies. The metaphysical principles that govern Spirit mean it can only have a very brief existence in this physical realm. Life provides an avenue or vessel for certain, specific lessons or certain, specific dimensions of Spirit's evolution. The fulfillment of its soul contract, that can only be learned in the physical.

Carissa Schumacher: I don't believe matter and Spirit are separate. They're both energy. One is simply lighter and less dense than the other. Matter is a lower-frequency energy with a greater density, giving us the perception that what we see is somehow real, but really it's all a holograph of dancing energy. Spirit aligns with and animates matter on every level, this physical body is just one of our nine light bodies, but the other eight are invisible from our physical plane. Enlightenment is becoming able to see and sense them as well as the interconnectedness in all things and the presence of Spirit within and beyond matter.

* * *

It hadn't occurred to me that there would be so many different answers to this or that there could be so many truths. However, by distilling what we've been given, and allowing a little poetic license, an incredibly beautiful image emerges:

The divine spark, the breath of God, aligns with matter, allowing the Creator to experience the created. Each life is a pulse, a wave of energy, and each of us is a Spirit surfing that wave. Like snowflakes each wave and every life is completely unique, and teaches us its own unique lesson. Our spirit is bound to our body by a silver cord just as a surfer is bound to his board by a cord. The length and quality of each wave, each ride through life, is defined by the soul contract that each of our individual spirits comes into life with.

We are Spirit surfers riding on the waves of creation.

We are creation experiencing itself.

Chapter 26

What Is the Force Binding Atoms to Create Matter?

Science has taught us that atoms break down into a host of subatomic particles in a complex dance of forces and charges, but the energy of the proton at the core of every atom has remained constant since the big bang almost fourteen billion years ago, and will remain so for trillions more years to come. Can Spirit give us an insight into how something so tiny could maintain such a dynamic and stable force over such a massive span of time?

AM: *What is the force that binds atoms together to create matter?*

Hollister Rand: Through my work as a medium, I've learned that the frequency of love is the most powerful force in the universe and that it's what's waiting for us all beyond this life. It creates stasis here in the physical realm, a constant force working to bring imbalance into balance. Maybe it's also the force binding everything together.

Lisa Williams: I'm not being given an answer to that. My sense is that it's energy, but exactly what kind of energy, I don't really know.

Jeffrey Wands: The power of creation.

Demi of California Psychics: The divine force of Spirit, the essence of creation. It's a light force, a matrix that holds and binds everything together. When I was studying chemistry, I learned that on the subatomic level everything's constantly moving. I'd always imagine what would happen if it stopped, would everything just drop to nothing? No matter what it is, it's just the movement in the atoms that make things appear solid to us when in reality they're holographic. We're living in a holographic dimension full of possibilities, and that always brings me back to the thought that all of this has been created, it's an act of creation, the divine force of Spirit at play?

Eden of California Psychics: They're showing me an endless wall of equations, but I couldn't begin to tell you what they are. There are gazillions of letters and numbers. Now they're showing me a nebula. It almost looks like a white puff of cloud that has tremendous energy in it. Just like a cloud, you can see it, but you can't touch it.

James of California Psychics: I get no sense of it from Spirit.

Antony Galvan: In this dimension, maybe it's time. It allows the vibration, the wave forms of electricity and magnetism that shape the structure of matter, to spread and fill space. They flow through the cosmos in a never-ending ocean of currents, changing the structure of everything they pass through and ultimately returning to their source.

Thomas John: Every piece of matter is energy, from the subatomic to the galactic. Everything is a pulse or waves of energy, pieces of a vast, infinite light that creates the physical dimension. There are infinite other dimensions we can't envision from within this one, but they are all bound by the same unifying principle.

Carissa Schumacher: While science might laugh at this, the answer is love. The forces of divine masculine and divine feminine merge in this sacred union. Every subatomic particle, atom, cell, and galaxy within our universe was birthed from the merging of the masculine divine, the creative seed of consciousness, and the feminine divine, the infinite womb of the nothingness that everything came from. That's how the primordial pulse of the universe began, in an act of love and passion, creation without agendas and boundaries.

* * *

Again, our panel presents a wide range of answers that paint an intriguing picture. Are we being given the challenge to see things differently? In art, the impressionists and then the modernists destroyed the classical style of representative and illustrative art that preceded it, so is Spirit here challenging us to look at the poetic rather than empirical?

Love, the divine force of Source brought about creation. It started with the big singularities, time, gravity and the big bang, then it moved right into the dualities of electricity and magnetism, which both dance to time's drum beat. This physical realm is an act of creation where creation can experience itself, but at its heart creation is love, thus the force at the heart of every proton is a manifestation of the power of love.

Chapter 27

What's the Experience of Spirit without Matter?

I'm convinced that our spirits, our essence, our souls, exist beyond our death. Since no one gets out of here alive, we'll all end up back where we came from, so what's it really like being there?

AM: *What's the experience of Spirit without matter?*

Hollister Rand: I'm not convinced that it is ever without matter. Spirit is just on a different plane, like light, love, thought, and thought-forms. In every connection I've made, and that's many, Spirit always describes death as a rebirth and the experience of passing over as a beautiful transition to a place of light and love. Spirit without matter becomes pure love.

Lisa Williams: After the body dies, the spirit continues experiencing the lessons of love and hate in the next dimension, continuing the process of growth between its lives here. These lessons learned are used to influence and guide those in this dimension and help ensure we're constantly living a better life.

Jeffrey Wands: It's pure consciousness, floating free, totally unconfined by matter. Spirits feel the emotions we're going through here and can make us feel things that they went through when they were here. For instance, if they died of cancer or a head trauma, you can tap into it and feel what they went through so you'll understand it, but they're no longer feeling it in a physical sense. They're beyond pain.

Demi of California Psychics: Purest joy! It's like the biggest smile, the joy of children at play, or the way certain songs lift your spirit, but more so.

Eden of California Psychics: Pure Spirit would be a thought-form, but they're telling me Spirit's essence is matter, just in a completely different dimension. They're asking me to give you the example of fabric, if matter in this dimension is like a heavy brocade, Spirit is like the finest gauze.

James of California Psychics: Spirit just is. It's a vibration, like listening to music. It resonates. I believe we all have a soul note. Pick your favorite six songs, and you'll find that they all have the same keynote, your soul note. When we pass, we transfer over to our highest spiritual vibration, but it isn't separate from who we are because we're all notes in a Spirit symphony.

Antony Galvan: I've experienced going beyond matter, being completely unshackled. I saw what an infinitesimally small fraction of the possibilities of existence there are in our time and matter based reality. It's a minuscule component of what lies beyond: the pure consciousness.

Thomas John: It's very, very peaceful and much more evolved than our experience here. We have infinite knowledge when we're not in this physical dimension, but when we come here, we forget everything because our soul contracts demand we have to learn by experience. Life really is like a test we have to master, so we have to prove our ability to learn. When Spirit is not in a physical body, it's clear, focused, centered, and full of knowledge. If you were in Spirit on the other side, you wouldn't be asking these questions because you'd already be in the knowledge of all the answers and more. However, there's the absence of things, for example. There are no physical sensations. It's almost like thought-focused existence.

Carissa Schumacher: Spirit without matter is unbridled light energy. Matter is the dense light energy of creation bound by time in a constant vibrational state. Spirit inhabits and transcends both matter and time, existing in a state similar to dreams, where the past and future all melt into the present. When Spirit leaves the body, it reenters that timeless state. Both the spirits of the departed and people who've had near-death experiences describe it as a fluid dance of returning to a harmonic, unconditionally loving space of higher consciousness, the Source, pure love. They always say it's like going home. It's also important to remember that this state is always accessible in our waking life when we lift the veils through meditation and contemplation.

* * *

This question inspired a far more unified set of answers, giving us a clear sense from Spirit of what it'll feel like when we pass over and what it feels like in the next dimension: We'll experience return home to a place of the purest joy. There, floating in an endless ocean of limitless knowledge and unconditional love, we'll be able to contemplate and absorb the lessons of this life while we prepare our soul contracts for the next one.

Chapter 28

Is Spirit Bound by Time, and How Does It Navigate Time?

We've learned that Spirit exists beyond all physical boundaries, but what about the big one: time. Everything in our dimension is defined by the dance of energy in the temple of time. In this physical realm, time really is the first dimension. Without it, there is no movement, and without movement, matter can't form. So without time's drumbeat, there is nothing, but what about Spirit?

AM: *Is Spirit bound by time, and how does it navigate time?*

Hollister Rand: Time is the most challenging thing to deal with being a medium. The spirits don't talk to me in time or use time references. They always give me information in the present tense, as if it's happening now, but it could have happened twenty years ago. Time and time of death have nothing to do with Spirit. They don't honor their time of death and want us to know that there is no time in death because they exist beyond time. They supersede time and are asking us to live our lives in that same way here. We live our lives with a "to do" list, but the spirits want us to live with a "to be" list. Being is not a time-based concept.

In terms of navigating time, I see spirits constantly showing up at the right time, but there are no watches there. My own guide tells me that they're called by thoughts and connections. Our thoughts are like phone calls, triggering a network that always delivers the message. That's the connection that brings Spirit through.

Lisa Williams: Gosh no, Spirit's absolutely not bound by time. Time is just one of matter's governing restrictions, but Spirit doesn't have any physicality, so it isn't subject to any of those restrictions. Spirit doesn't have to navigate time because there simply isn't any element of time for it. They come when it's necessary to communicate, like us going to another country and automatically being in that time zone. When we call Spirit, we raise our vibrations, and spirits lower theirs to come down toward us. They will never cross our boundaries and always connect in the middle. They can communicate at any point because they're always aware of our thoughts and feelings. They'll always reach out to us when we need them, it can be in the middle of the night, in a dream, waking in the morning, anytime at all.

AM: *When Spirit comes back to us, is it an individual's spirit or is it Spirit wearing the face of an individual we recognize?*

Lisa Williams: Yes, that's exactly what it is. That spirit will have had several lives before incarnating as the person we knew. Since it doesn't have any physical body when it comes through to a medium like myself, it has to appear in a form that the client will recognize. My grandfather's a classic example. He died at eighty-three without any hair, but he hated going bald. When he decided to come back, he came back to me looking younger with all his hair. Of course, even though he appeared to me, he didn't have that physical body. He manifested that vision, choosing how he wanted to look. They come back the way they want to be remembered and, of course, how you'll remember them.

Jeffrey Wands: Time as we know it is meaningless to the spirits, and they don't have to navigate time because they can be anywhere and everywhere at once. I've often been woken up by them because they don't seem to bother about time. The plane they're on is so different that they completely forget how time exists for us.

Demi of California Psychics: Time doesn't exist for Spirit, so it isn't bound by time, and it navigates it in an instant because it's everywhere all at once.

Eden of California Psychics: Spirit is not bound by time nor does it operate in time. Spirit is more like a thought-form, it understands time, but it's not subject to it. "Navigating time" is a term we use because we're in this physicality, which is defined by time, but Spirit doesn't experience time like that. For Spirit, it's all inclusive, and everything happens at once. They think a thought, and they're there, and then think another, and they're there.

James of California Psychics: There's certainly a distortion between time here and how time changes when we return to Spirit. When I'm working with Spirit, time seems to change, but I don't know how or why. Everything from Spirit seems sped up, faster, when you're in it, but I can't really say if Spirit's bound by time or how it navigates it.

Antony Galvan: No, that's just simple physics. Time is really just a limiter of this dimension. The minute we transcend it and go into higher dimensions, we're no longer bound by the rules and limitations of this dimension.

Thomas John: Spirit exists in a lot of different dimensions and a lot of different times simultaneously. Time manifests the physical, but it's almost an illusion. When Spirit is here, in body and in life, time is a tool to keep us on track. It creates the senses of urgency and completion that we need to accomplish and fulfill the challenges of our soul contracts. If we were eternal in this physical plane, we'd never finish anything because we could always do it tomorrow or in a millennium. Spirit inhabits multiple dimensions at once, which is why some of our dreams are so real. How many times have you woken from a dream feeling like you've been in a very familiar place that you don't know? Through Spirit, we can be in other dimensions, in other eras in the past, or in the future. The spirits know time rules our physical dimension, so when they do come through to connect, they're aware you're here in time.

AM: *How do they navigate time to get here from there?*

Thomas John: Spirits are in knowledge and thus know where you are in your journey in this dimension. If they want to communicate with you, they know how to come into this space-time dimension, and equally, if you reach out to them, they can reach back to give you a message.

Carissa Schumacher: When Spirit is not bound to a physical object or body, it exists in a state of nonlinear time, where all things occur within the present. This is the true essence of time. We just cannot comprehend or experience it in this way until we raise our vibrations and reach beyond the veils of our human form. This is why mindfulness is so important. The past does not exist. The future does not exist. Everything, all past lives, future lives, and this life, occur and exist within the singularity of this very moment. The same is true for Spirit. Spirit is lighter and thus can maneuver through time and space with a different, purer frequency.

Spirit navigates time as we navigate dreams, there's no thinking involved in the process. It goes back into the past, into the future, and through the portal of the present all at once, but it has to expend an extraordinary amount of energy to break through the space-time continuum into the human psyche. The easiest way for Spirit to communicate with us is through dreams, where we can access expanded forms of consciousness beyond the veils.

AM: *So can we see through these veils and connect with Spirit in our waking life?*

Carissa Schumacher: Yes, to commune with Spirit, stay present within the present. Spirit guides and guardian angels speak to us through the heart in the poetic spirit language of energy and emotions. The sacred wisdom of their truth always resonates most clearly in the moments when we clear our minds, open the gateway to our intuition, and allow ourselves to simply and gently listen.

* * *

Here we have a unanimous accord: Spirit is completely free of time, existing in a dimension beyond time and able to be anywhere at any time, all the time. This explains why my father returned with a thousand-strong army of relatives who stretched across the eons, yet came as one to welcome him.

Time it seems is at the very core of this dimension, everything that *is*, be it sub-atomic or galactic, marches to its drum beat, so it makes perfect sense that Spirit exists in a dimension beyond time.

Chapter 29

Is There Other Life in the Universe, and Does It Share the Same Spirit?

What of the rest of our universe? We've detected the sugars that form the basis of life floating around a young star just 400 light-years away, and 750 light-years away an embryonic star is literally blasting water out of its poles. These and countless other new discoveries strengthen the possibility, even probability, that many stars have life-giving and sustaining 'Goldilocks Zones' around them. We've all grown up with stories of aliens, from Roswell to E.T., so I wanted to see if our experts get a sense of whether there's other life in our universe.

AM: *Is there other life in the universe, and does it share the same Spirit?*

Hollister Rand: Spirit and energy are inseparable. Thinking of Spirit as energy, we know everything inanimate or animate is made of atoms, so it has and emits energy. That means it's all a part of the expression of creation, so if there is other life out there, it's a part of the same Spirit.

Lisa Williams: Yes, and I believe it also has Spirit. Personally, I haven't had that connection, but someone I absolutely trust has. She communicated more than once with extra-planetary life and said the experience was both incredible and life changing.

Jeffrey Wands: I haven't experienced it, but I've learned not to question anything doing what I do. However I think it would have to be involved with Spirit because it's a form of life, and thus consciousness.

Demi of California Psychics: Yes, and it's not just one, it's many. Energetically, I feel we've been blind by thinking we're the only ones. We're all little experiments of life happening at different times and on planes throughout the universe over billions of years. Stars and planets have come and gone, but life, the divine force, keeps taking hold wherever it can. My sense is that it's the divine plan, creation experiencing the created in an endless series of Spiritual boot camps for learning, growing, and awareness.

Eden of California Psychics: Yes, we all come from Spirit, which is also the Great Intelligence. There's certainly other life out there, some is more advanced, some more primitive. Not better or worse, just different.

James of California Psychics: A lot of mediums have told me that they've experienced things that are of alien or extraterrestrial origin, and they're absolutely convinced of it. If there are other beings, I hope they can help us and that we welcome them rather than shoot them!

AM: *Are they getting a unified message through these contacts?*

James of California Psychics: I know one who claims she's seen beings. Invariably what comes through is the sense of caution about the gift of mediumship because it can be used the wrong way, as with remote viewing in wartime. She said that they're very concerned that we're not ready to do the things we're doing right now, like cloning, which can create armies. It seems their message is more on the side of peace and harmony, not unlike Spirit. I guess if they're advanced enough to cover those distances of time and space, then they're a lot more spiritually evolved. So maybe they're trying to save us from some unseen horrors in our future.

Antony Galvan: Absolutely, it's all made from the same stuff. Like the oceans: different waves, same water.

Thomas John: There's other life on this earth dimension, for sure. There are life energies connected with the sun and every star, so there is definitely the energy of life throughout our Universe. There's also life in other dimensions that we can't access. It's not life in terms of Homo sapiens on another planet, but energies that are highly evolved and highly intellectual, far more evolved than us. I'm being told that within our galaxy there are star beings. We just haven't discovered them yet.

AM: *And that life, does it have Spirit?*

Thomas John: Yes, it has Spirit and it is Spirit. Some of those energies, those beings, have massively long life spans and are able to go in between the physical and spiritual planes.

Carissa Schumacher: If by "other life" you mean other organisms that are self-aware, intelligent life as we understand it, then yes. There are beings of all levels of intelligence and evolution, including beings of such great intelligence that they can interact through multidimensional worlds and realities, like Spirit. Many ancient and indigenous societies referred to them as the Star People, the Sky People, and the Shining Ones. There's life everywhere within our universe, outside our universe, and every which way in between.

Spirit is the synthesis between the small percentage of matter in our universe and the larger percentage that we cannot see unless we lift the veils to see beyond with intuition. This larger, hidden percentage is what we feel when we open our hearts to Spirit and embrace the vibrations and energies of the web of life connecting and unifying us all. These two percentages couple to create everything and the nothing. There is no separation between life, matter, and Spirit, they're all one and the same. Thus, all things are created of Spirit, and all things are Spirit.

* * *

That's a resounding yes from everyone, and two who know people who've had first hand experiences. I've also spoken to people whom I absolutely trust who've seen UFOs and are absolutely certain about it.

Around the time of the Roswell incident, Carl Jung published the results of his twenty years researching UFOs. In his interview with the *New York Herald Tribune* published on July 30, 1958, he said, "I can only say for certain that these things are not a mere rumor. Something has been seen." He went on to say that the reported crafts and their movements were far beyond our engineering ability. Today, the Internet and cable TV are full of UFO stories and tales of ancient aliens, but our current understanding of physics says it's impossible to travel across the massive distances through space. At the speed of light, it would take over 27,000 years to get to the center of our galaxy, the Milky Way, or 2.5 million years to get here from our nearest neighbor, the Andromeda galaxy, so there's no way we're popping over there for the weekend.

I believe this quote by Carl Sagan (1934–1996) sums up our experts' answers perfectly: "We are a way for the Cosmos to know itself."

Chapter 30

Does Spirit Exist Beyond the Bounds of This Universe?

Our universe burst into existence 13.7 billion years ago. What it exploded into was obviously here before the big bang, and is also what our universe is expanding into. Whatever it is, it remains beyond the vision of our instruments, but maybe Spirit has ability to see it.

AM: *Does Spirit exist beyond the bounds of this universe?*

Hollister Rand: As far as I've seen, but I have not seen the end of it. Spirit appears to be boundless. We're limited by our own sense of boundaries, but I'm not sure what the limits of Spirit are because I have not seen them.

Lisa Williams: Absolutely! I'm certain there's more out there than we can imagine. Look at the size and scale of our universe, it's impossible to think there isn't more. We'd have to be really naïve to think we're all there is.

Jeffrey Wands: Quantum physics would suggest so, but honestly I don't know.

Demi of California Psychics: Yes, without question. Within the astral traveling I've done, I can say there is so much more out there. While channeling Spirit I've always been told we are just one of many. Spirit is infinite, so it must exist beyond, before, and after our universe.

Eden of California Psychics: First you have to believe there are bounds to this universe, but there are not. There is no edge to the universe because it keeps manifesting and growing. Scientists discover more galaxies, but they were always there. Electricity was here when Moses walked the earth, but he didn't know it or how to harness it. In the same way, we have to learn to look through a new lens to see the extent of Spirit because the old one simply can't reveal it.

James of California Psychics: Spirit is inseparable from the divine, the Source. It's everywhere, here, now, before, and after. It's both what we sprang from and what is beyond.

Antony Galvan: Of course. Spirit exists wherever it seeks itself.

Thomas John: I'm being told yes, that there are limitless universes and dimensions, and Spirit is in all of them. It can go between universes and dimensions, and being in one doesn't mean it isn't in another simultaneously. Spirit can have multiple iterations in the same dimension or universe, but it's entirely possible to be in another dimension at the same time.

Carissa Schumacher: Yes, there are infinite universes and infinite dimensions—more than we can imagine. Everything that exists is Spirit, so other universes must inherently be Spirit, too.

* * *

That's another resounding yes: Spirit is both before and beyond. It stretches through the endlessness of the multiverse and is present in the nothingness from which everything sprang. Perhaps that nothingness is the Source where Spirit resides?

Chapter 31

Where Does Spirit Go?

Stories of reincarnation are as old as the first religions, and in many of the spiritual teachings they are treated as completely matter of fact. Even within our small group of interviewees, we've heard how Starlette's young daughter recounted a past life. If we keep returning to learn life's lessons here on earth, where does our spirit go when it finally completes its soul-cycle incarnations, and it's time to leave all this behind?

AM: *Where does Spirit go after completing its soul-cycle incarnations here?*

Hollister Rand: One spirit talked to me of a place with no fragments, a place where there is wholeness, where everything makes sense, and all is understood. I also think there are many steps along the way. I've been shown many frequencies from the other side, full of sounds and colors that act as latitude and longitude, each taking us to a certain vibrational space. The other side is much bigger than we can imagine.

AM: *Do you think that a "place with no fragments" refers to us being fragments of greater souls, as suggested in "Many Lives, Many Masters" by Brian Weiss, MD?"*

Hollister Rand: I don't want to put too much meaning on that statement, but a spirit once said to me, "I have met my many selves." I'm still thinking about that one. The idea of fragments, parts, and things coming together and creating a whole is where I think we're headed: A place where everything's in perfect balance. Love perfected. A place where we're being called into wholeness.

Lisa Williams: I believe that once we've done our incarnations and have chosen not to do this anymore, we go on to be pure Spirit, master guides.

We help the Spirits closer to the physical world, those that are still connected to the earth plane, by bringing forth guidance and love.

Jeffrey Wands: Ultimately, to a higher presence, but since people aren't perfect, we keep on coming back here and trying to get it right.

AM: *Have you ever experienced a specific soul or spirit reenter life in your work?*

Jeffrey Wands: Yes, I had a client come to me whose sister had died when they were kids. They'd been playing in the garden when the sister ran into the clothesline, got caught up in it, and strangled herself. The other sister wasn't able to save her in time and always felt responsible. Years later, when she had her first child, a little girl, she named her after her sister. Well, one day when this child was around three, she suddenly said, "Don't you remember we used to play that game as kids, and this was that song we'd always sing?" Then she started singing that song. Nobody in the world knew about it except the two sisters, and in that moment my client realized that her sister had come back to her as her daughter.

Demi of California Psychics: I feel Spirit goes into ever-flowing, constantly moving cycles, processing the experiences and lessons learned in life. Souls are constantly returning to and from here, so Spirit itself is being transformed through its experience here.

Eden of California Psychics: It's not a place sitting on a cloud somewhere; it's more like returning to a state of being. I remember when I was sick with a 106-degree fever as a child that I asked if I was going to die, and Spirit told me I wasn't, but as an obstinate kid I demanded to know what I'd take with me if I did. The answer was my mind. I realized then that our brain is just an earthly vessel to contain the mind, but it's a separate thing. Our minds are part of our souls, our own spirits, and what we return to Spirit with. Where then does Spirit ultimately go? I don't know, but I'd guess to Source.

James of California Psychics: Since we're all part of the same Source energy, as are our loved ones who've passed on, I imagine that once Spirit has completed its incarnations here, it returns to Source.

Antony Galvan: Into an infinite expansion. It just keeps evolving infinitely.

Thomas John: To another dimension of learning and knowledge, but it's not a physical dimension at all. There's really no stopping point where somebody says "okay, you've learned everything, you've mastered everything, you know everything, so now you can stop." It's more of an endless state of unfolding, a dimension we can't get to, and one that isn't physical but more of a soul, spiritual, and energetic existence. It's a destination, a place of absolute unity. Within that dimension, there are billions or trillions of smaller dimensions, where different soul purposes play out or different groups of souls gather to accomplish and move things. Our universe is one tiny projection of it. There are many others that are physical by nature, but very different from ours, that are also connected to that spiritual center.

Carissa Schumacher: After achieving the mastery of this human existence, our spirits ascend to a higher form and dimension of consciousness without limitations. There, the spirits join the ranks of the Ascended Masters and spirit guides who create the divine blueprint of life, interacting through the vibrations of light and sound. As a spirit ascends higher in its vibration, it becomes stripped of its individuation and reunites with Source. Eventually, the spirit completely dissolves, becoming one with the Alpha and the Omega, the All and the None.

* * *

Once more, we have unanimous agreement from those who work with Spirit: Once an individual spirit finishes its soul-cycle incarnations here, it ascends to a higher level of being, to a place beyond fragments, to become one with Spirit and return to the ever unfolding, ever present, Source.

The concept of levels of ascension, or heaven, is echoed in almost every wisdom teaching, from the biblical angels to the Judaic Shamayim and the New Age Ascended Masters. A visualization of this could be that Source, the place of no fragments, is like the great unknown that the universe is expanding into, and was here before the big bang. We, the fragments, like the stars and galaxies, are all inside it, and as our spirit grows, it moves outward into more expansive layers of being, eventually reuniting with Source.

Chapter 32

Is Destiny a Script We Can't Change?

We've all experienced déjà vu, the sense that we've been somewhere before or done something already. Precognitive dreams point toward time being nonlinear, as do the visions of psychics who see things that haven't happened. How could that be possible if time is linear? If time isn't linear, then maybe everything has already happened, and our experience in life is like riding a roller-coaster, the ride is always the same, but each spirit experiences it in their own way. If that's the case, then destiny really is written, but what can we do about it in this incarnation?

AM: *Is destiny a script we can't change?*

Hollister Rand: What the spirits have shown me is that we choose the people with whom we grow up before we come into this life. We choose our experiences in life but not necessarily the actual circumstances by which those experiences come. I work a lot with parents who've lost children, and I can honestly say I don't believe these parents and children come into this world with a destiny to suffer such great tragedies. However, their souls may have contracts and agreements with one another about what they need to learn in this lifetime. You could say there's a level of destiny in the soul's requirements and what Spirit needs to get out of a certain incarnation. That'll bring about the circumstances through which we learn and make our choices, which is where free will comes in. A tragedy in someone's life can yield different results. You can expand into it, allowing it to open you into an incredible spiritual unfolding, or contract into blaming others for your loss, railing against the injustice of it all and hating the world. Free will not only determines how we respond to tragedy, but it also affects every other living being in our world. The decisions we make every day absolutely change things, but what we experience was decided and agreed upon before we came here.

AM: *So there's a level of eventuality. It's not as predetermined as saying it's already happened—you're just experiencing it now.*

Hollister Rand: There's a destination that has destiny in it, but there are also choices we have along the way allowing us to define what route we'll take to get there.

Lisa Williams: We can change our destiny. We have a life contract that our spirit guides hold. It's important to maintain it because we've chosen it for a reason, for the lessons we have to learn. When we see clearly where we are and the course we want to be on, I believe we can create change through communication and connection with our spirit guides. Of course, we have lessons to complete, but by learning from them we can change our path to a certain degree.

Jeffrey Wands: Yes, I believe we can alter our destiny through the journey of life, but not when it comes to our death.

AM: *So we do have the power of free will?*

Jeffrey Wands: Yes, believe it or not, we can absolutely screw things up.

Demi of California Psychics: Before we enter this life, there is a contract made, but once you arrive here it's up to you how you experience your life. We're set on a track, but it comes down to your mind-set, how you think and behave. In every action is the potential for good or creating backlashes. Ultimately, you're going to the same place: back into Spirit. Free will defines how many detours you take to get there.

Eden of California Psychics: We can to a certain extent because we live in a world of duality. It's a yes and no answer. If you look at it from a broader perspective, it's all a temporary experience even if you live to be a hundred. Sure, some people are going to go earlier than others, but

I think that's a preincarnation choice. So are things predestined? What they're telling me is that everything's already happened, which takes away the idea of free will, and that's a pretty scary. They're showing me it's a loop, a cycle. Even though the universe seems to be expanding, it's all already happened. Time in the physical world just makes it seem like it's a singular linear event, but all this has happened countless times before.

James of California Psychics: We have soul contracts prior to birth, as well as soul mates, and twin flames. In terms of personal destiny, your check-in and check-out times are set, as are those you're destined to come in contact with. Husbands, wives, children, friends, and enemies are all here to teach us. We're all here to learn from one another at the right time and lift one another up to the next level. We can change destiny with each decision we make by our own free will, but ego is difficult to get over and often leads us down horrible pathways, bringing us back to karma. On a brighter note, synchronicity, which we all recognize, is destiny at play.

Antony Galvan: If you'd asked me this a year ago, I'd have been more ambivalent, but now I absolutely believe in destiny in terms of our earthbound existence. Our spirits do seem to agree on certain events before they guide us into this life. Free will, I'm not so sure about. A recent scientific study of the brain showed that even when people try to be spontaneous, their minds have always made the choice they think is theirs a split-second beforehand.

AM: *I believe that's the study that inspired Sam Harris's book on free will.*

Antony Galvan: Yes, as Buddha said, "We suffer the illusion of choice." Our ego wants to feel that it's consciously in control of our environment, but really everything is happening exactly the way it's meant to. Everything that's happened was meant to be, there's never been a thing that shouldn't have happened.

AM: *Considering the atrocities committed by our species, that's a scary thought.*

Antony Galvan: Yes, it is, but you can't change events. You can only change how you respond to them. Free will is whether you react, which is thoughtless, or you respond, which is thoughtful. If you allow your inner state to be the victim of outside circumstances, you're forever going to be tossed about like a rag doll. To quote Buddha once more: "Outside circumstances are merely adverse or favorable, true happiness comes from within."

Thomas John: We can absolutely alter our destiny. We have certain soul contracts that we agree to before we come here, but we don't have to stick to them. It's like we make certain agreements on the big-picture items, but how we get there can be done in many different ways. A lot depends on free will and chance. For example, we may have a soul contract that in this lifetime, we're going to help others, but it could be done in multiple ways. Rarely do we get assigned a specific job or anything like that, but we have soul contracts with those people who are going to be important in our lives. I've never been told that every little thing is planned out.

AM: *So there's a destination, but how we get there is our choice?*

Thomas John: Yes.

Carissa Schumacher: Prior to birth, we all create soul contracts, binding energetic agreements involving not only our own selves, but also those we're to have major interactions with, such as our parents, teachers, partners, and so on. Our spirit self creates this blueprint as a template for how our unique divine life-force, or shakti, fits into the greater web of life. Within this blueprint, you also choose circumstances, experiences, and karmic lessons to master and learn, so you can rebalance your karma and ascend to higher dimensions of consciousness. These can include past-life issues that need to be resolved and agreements set up with others to help you within that process. The spirit self is always present at the chessboard of life, watching the maneuvers and players in the game, but here on the board of life, we can't see that bigger picture. We're blinded by the veils of illusion and the false perception of separation between both self and other, between self and the divine. The veils stop us from seeing the divinity inherent in our own humanity and realizing that every experience and encounter in life is a lesson we chose to neutralize our karma and ascend to our highest vibration.

AM: *So destiny is scripted, predestined?*

Carissa Schumacher: Yes, yet while destiny is a blueprint, it only presents us with the events into which our lessons are woven. We can reorchestrate certain outcomes by awakening to our higher self, releasing ego and consciously raising our vibration. That will allow us to align ourselves with Spirit and begin the journey of enlightenment and self-mastery.

* * *

Again, we received a clear set of answers. All that is has already happened before. This moment, the here and now, is just our turn at experiencing it. Destiny defines both our destination, the challenges on the path, and the choices we must make to get there. Freedom is how we respond to those challenges while on the journey to our own true destiny, the reunion with Spirit.

Chapter 33

Karma

Karma, it's a term I've heard used as if it's some kind of retributive force out to bite you in the ass if you've been bad. What it is really, how does it work and do we carry it forward from this life to the next?

AM: *How does karma work? Does it affect Spirit, and is it changeable?*

Hollister Rand: The spirits don't talk to me about karma. They speak about legacy. Legacy is what we leave behind and give to the next generations. These legacies can run the gamut from fortune to abuse to alcoholism. I talk about this in my book because it's one of the keys to really understanding and claiming one's freedom. One of the more interesting sessions I had was with several generations of an entire family, living and in spirit, who'd been affected by alcoholism. The ones in spirit all passed in alcohol-related situations—even those who were not drinkers. One young man who'd never touched the stuff was killed by a drunk driver. To us, this looks like karma, what goes around, comes around, or that we're stuck in some sort of wheel, but what the spirits talk about is the freedom from legacy. I'm aligning legacy with karma, but not as it may be understood in any religious sense. Legacy is about getting stuck in patterns, and the spirits are constantly sending through messages encouraging us to free ourselves from it and end any ingrained familial beliefs about how our experience here should play out. My sense is that both legacy and karma aren't things we have to keep repeating or go through over and over again.

Lisa Williams: I do believe it's important for all of us to know that karma does come around and is part of our learning. It's put in our pathway to help us grow and get out of our egotistical self. It's very important for us.

AM: *Does it affect Spirit?*

Lisa Williams: I believe Spirit understands more than us why karma is around and how it can pass from life to life, so it's certainly aware of it and its effects.

Jeffrey Wands: It affects us more than Spirit. There's a kind of cause and effect that leads to recurrences taking place, usually of things we need to learn to grow and evolve. We can try to avoid them, but like a boomerang, they come back to us.

Demi of California Psychics: Yes, it affects Spirit, but it's absolutely changeable. I've experienced people coming to see me with a great deal of pain for things they've done, but in the expression of heartfelt regret and honest sorrow, they can energetically wipe the slate clean. Spirit is a lot more forgiving than we are, but if you don't own your responsibility in a given situation, you'll force the divine to bring it up again and again until you really learn the lesson. That isn't just saying the words, it's feeling it in the depth of your heart, with your whole essence, and forgiving yourself. Wiping your slate clean is much better than paying the penance. If you don't make the right decisions in this lifetime, the consequences will be pushed into another, so deal with it now!

Eden of California Psychics: In the sense of what goes around, comes around? I don't believe in such a thing as punitive karma, like you destroyed that family generations ago and now you must pay for what you did. Karma is like a mirror—the energy we put out to the world, all our energy, and even our thoughts have an impact. Karma teaches us the lessons of the way we've been living, so with the right attitude, it'll teach us about ourselves and show us how through change, we can get closer to the divine. Don't look at it as seeing what's wrong, use it as a tool to learn how to evolve and reconnect with your highest potential.

James of California Psychics: There are many different levels. On the physical level, if you let negativity build up and get you into a negative state of mind, you'll attract like for like. If your energy is high, strong, and positive, then that's exactly what you'll draw to you. On the higher level of Spirit, I'm not sure. I know from my experience of past lives that things get carried forward to be resolved, but I'm not sure if they affect Spirit or if Spirit is simply giving them back like a riddle to be unraveled this time around. That, of course, answers the part about it being changeable. It absolutely is, and changing it should always be our spiritual priority.

Antony Galvan: Karma is a very advanced notion, but once you wake up to it and embrace it in your heart, you become fully responsible for every decision you make. Karma isn't an unwritten law that says, "You hurt me so you're going to get hurt." It's a radical responsibility for yourself in every moment. It's understanding that your every action is interconnected to everything else. If you truly embrace it, it's a commitment to constantly being the best you can be, living righteously, and truly doing unto others as you would have them do unto you.

AM: *But if destiny is already written, doesn't that make karma almost irrelevant?*

Antony Galvan: Karma is the richness in destiny's story. Karma is the opportunity within destiny for you to become your highest self, to awaken, become, and witness your God self. You could say that if the script of destiny is already written, a contract has been made with Spirit, and then Karma provides the challenges you must overcome to grow into your God self.

Thomas John: There is karma in our soul contracts, the agreements we make with our soul tribe, our loved ones, and our spirit guides, so by definition that becomes our karma. It can be very positive, and we can do things here to shift it. For example, if we have the karma to go through certain negative experiences, we can minimize the impact of them by learning the lessons they bring quickly. The key is in growing and changing, and the best way to do that is with awareness, and working to change ourselves.

Karma is almost like our spiritual genetics. For example, if your genetics dictate that you have diabetes, you can minimize the effects once you're aware of it. If you never pay attention to it, you'll be the victim of it, but it's always your choice how you deal with it. We can do spiritual work on our own to shift or detach us from certain legacies or lineages of karma, and that is where our free will comes in. When we raise our vibration through diet, meditation, and doing spiritual work on ourselves, we shift our behavior, and thus, we shift our karma.

Carissa Schumacher: Karma isn't some divine form of retribution or punishment. It's just the energetic cycles of action and reaction. For every action, there's an equal and opposite reaction, what you put out is what comes back. Karma is neither good nor bad, judge nor jury. It's always neutral, allowing us to learn and master our soul's lessons and ascend into our own enlightenment.

We create ripples in the pool by casting a stone into it. Those ripples carry through from life to life, incarnation to incarnation, until we learn how to neutralize them and bring ourselves back into tranquility again. In this physical realm of polarities, good karma is generated when your thoughts, words, and deeds emanate from a genuine place of love and compassion from within your heart. That doesn't mean just doing good deeds over giving or martyring yourself. It has to be a deep inner transformation, an alignment with your spirit's truth, to generate the positive karma necessary.

Bad karma is sending a negative energy out into the universe: anger, fear, greed, or any of the seven so-called sins. It's all the disharmonious thoughts, words, and deeds that go against the universal energies of love and harmony in this life and in past lives. They replay as karmic warps that create shadow blocks over your seven chakras, the seven gateways to the Womb-Grail, and the Seven Seals of Revelation. That negativity is held within your light bodies as a charged, vibrational vortex called a samskara.

AM: *I've never heard that term before. Can you explain what samskara is?"*

Carissa Schumacher: Samskara can be likened to scars upon the soul. Some are superficial, and some are very deep. The more a negative behavior is reinforced, the deeper the scar gets. They distort and block our divine-energy flow, ultimately leading to the generation of veils, ego, and mind chatter that prevent us from connecting with our higher self. They build up behind the wall of complacency as pressures of everyday life allow us to resist and ignore our need to change. We can become conscious of them by taking personal responsibility for all that occurs within our lives, neutralizing our negative reactions in the face of adversity, and reviewing our behavioral patterns, attachments, and beliefs. Awareness is the first step to healing them.

AM: *How does one go about healing them?*

Carissa Schumacher: By witnessing and embracing all parts of self, the shadow and the light, then infusing compassion, patience, and love toward all areas of darkness, anger, or pain. Judging ourselves, blaming others, or trying to push aside energies that hurt and provoke us is like picking at a scab. It only escalates the karma. Witnessing, embracing, and transforming fear, anger, or pain into vulnerability and love neutralizes the energy of the samskara and allows us to break free from the cycle of karma. If we each turned inward to awaken and surrender to our higher truth, we'd neutralize our karma, and in helping others to do the same, we'd co-create heaven on earth.

AM: *What a beautiful concept. Thank you!*

* * *

These answers have given me a great insight into what karma is, how it works and how to ensure my actions and reactions remain in harmony with it.

Chapter 34

Source

"Source" is a word that came up several times in the later stages of these interviews, and it is a term I had not been familiar with before. I initially thought it had a bit of a *Star Wars,* "May the Force be with you," feel to it, yet all of our experts say that once a spirit finishes its soul-cycle incarnations here, it ascends to Source. Once the interview transcripts were completed, I realized I should have asked everyone about Source in the beginning, but it was hard to arrange a second round of interviews. So I just went back to Thomas John and Carissa Schumacher, as their answers have been so insightful, to ask if they'd give us a reading on Source from Spirit.

AM: *Can you give us your insight into Source?*

Thomas John: I'm being told that like time, Source is really an illusion we've created to give ourselves an understanding of creation. There's a very high-powered, energetic force that runs through everything that has a highly intellectual way of organizing, creating, and giving things destiny and purpose, but it's really just a force. It's not a living, breathing thing, but it's within all of us and everything in all the universes and all the dimensions beyond the farthest reaches of the imagination. It is the infinite.

Carissa Schumacher: The Source is ever present, living with and through us. It is the "what is" and the "what is not" from which everything came. It surrounds and permeates everything. It is before, after, and throughout all time. It is emptiness so vast that it is full and fullness so vast that it is empty. In it, form dissolves into formlessness and is reborn into form again. There are no veils, duality, or poles and opposites. It is the zero point.

As an energy, we recognize it in love, not just the feeling, but because the outcome of all love is creation. We can experience it in meditation, and we'll reunite with it in death. In Source, the "I am" becomes just "am." The soul's ultimate journey is uniting with the infinite Hu, the origin and completion of all.

* * *

This gives us a great sense of Source from Spirit, and as you'll see in the next section, the concept of a source is something that science is looking at from the opposite, empirical direction.

Section Four

Science and Reality

Chapter 35

Standing on the Shoulders of Giants

"The human mind is not capable of grasping the Universe. We are like a little child entering a huge library. The walls are covered to the ceilings with books in many different tongues. The child knows that someone must have written these books. It does not know who or how. It does not understand the languages in which they are written. But the child notes a definite plan in the arrangement of the books, a mysterious order which it does not comprehend, but only dimly suspects."

—*Albert Einstein*

We experience our time in this dimension as real, but what is reality? I believe it isn't possible to understand Spirit without examining reality itself, so for this section, I interviewed some of the giants of science. These men and women are the real explorers of our time, the ones truly going where no man has gone before, dedicating their lives to revealing the mysteries of the atom and the cosmos. What they're working on is radically altering our understanding of everything that is, and even that which is not.

We all know that science is constantly pushing back the veils of ignorance, revealing the truths of our physical reality. A hundred years ago, we only knew of just one galaxy, our own, but today we've counted around four hundred billion. We now know that the galaxies, the stars, the sun, the planets, and all the material stuff of the universe, including you and me, amounts to just 4 percent of its total weight and energy. The other 96 percent is made up of dark matter and dark energy. Even though scientific observation proves beyond doubt that they're both there, we have no idea of what they are.

Our instruments can see all the way out to the cosmic microwave background, the inside wall of the shock wave of the big bang, and the edge of our expanding universe, yet we have no idea what came before the big bang or what we're expanding into.

At the Large Hadron Collider in Switzerland, they're accelerating subatomic particles to almost the speed of light, and then smashing them into one another to re-create the forces of the big bang. The most publicized reason for this has been to identify the Higgs boson, the so-called God particle, which as you will read here has revealed an entirely new layer of mystery. Less heralded is the testing of the two main theories of subatomic physics: the standard model and supersymmetry. Every atom in our universe is constructed of just three things: electrons, protons, and neutrons. They in turn each contain seventeen different observed subatomic particles, but supersymmetry proposes an invisible quantum dimension that would allow for a mirrored set of particles matching the ones we know. If we can find a way to identify and observe this hidden dimension, it will totally change our understanding of reality, and it may give us the first clue to understanding dark matter and possibly even dark energy.

So despite science's ceaseless quest for certainty, it's confronted by the fact that we're afloat in a universe that is more mysterious than we could ever have imagined. So what does that have to do with Spirit? Well, it doesn't fit into the confines of science because science is the study of the "what is," the empirical, the measurable, and the repeatable, while Spirit is of the "what is not," the immeasurable. That means the two should be mutually exclusive. Yet in our reality, both are inextricably interwoven in our life experience, which as you will see through the eyes of our scientists, is incredibly mysterious.

Chapter 36

Dr. Maria Spiropulu and Dr Erik Verlinde

Maria Spiropulu, (MS, Harvard University, 1995, and PhD, Harvard, 2000) is a professor of physics at the California Institute of Technology and an experimental physicist. She has been researching elementary particles and their interactions over the past twenty years at Fermilab's Tevatron and is now doing the same research at the Large Hadron Collider (LHC) in Switzerland.

Erik Verlinde (PhD) is a Dutch theoretical physicist, string theorist and professor at the University of Amsterdam. The Verlinde Formula, which is important in conformal field theory and topological field theory, is named after him. His research deals with string theory, gravity, black holes, and cosmology. His theory of entropic gravity has garnered a lot of attention as a possible paradigm shift in fundamental physics. He works at the Institute for Theoretical Physics at the University of Amsterdam.

AM: *Thank you both for joining me for this interview. First, I'd like to get a picture of the forces at work within an atom. Maria, since your expertise is in the micro, what is the nature of subatomic particles, and what's the difference between them?*

Maria: The nature of the elementary subatomic particles is quantum. The difference between them is their quantum properties, their mass, and the way they interact with different forces. There are heavy particles and light particles (as in lightweight, not particles of light). In different configurations, the light particles make everything of everything—the galaxies, the stars, and everything we see. We understand the particles that make up the known 3 or

4 percent of the universe (everything in our current physical realm, space, time, gravity, and energy), and that won't change regardless of what we learn about the rest. For us scientists, the most interesting stuff is the stuff we can measure—all that other mysterious stuff can only be described with theoretical models. That means the possibilities of what it can be described as are infinite, while what we know is definitely what we know. There are genuinely mysterious things, like the weakly interacting massive particles (WIMPs). We know how or why they exist, but on them hinges answers about the way the universe works, so they could be described as being degrees of freedom that'll help us understand everything.

AM: *On the atomic scale, has a hydrogen atom been the same since the big bang?*

Maria: Yes! And it's the same atom of hydrogen here and at the edge of the universe. An electron is the same here as it is at the edge of the universe. Light is the same here and at the edge of the universe. It's amazing to me that everything is so consistent because there is nothing that says it has to be.

AM: *So on the subatomic scale, will reality hold together infinitely?*

Maria: By our current calculations, it looks like the proton at its core will hold together for another hundred thousand billion billion billion years, so we're still in its early infancy.

Erik: Atoms have been torn apart many times, in exploding stars, for instance.

Maria: Atoms decay, and get re-created.

Erik: There was also a moment back in the universe's early history when there weren't any atoms, there were only charged protons. You couldn't even see because electrons and protons weren't together, so light couldn't travel through them.

Maria: The universe was a dense plasma soup that nothing could get through.

AM: *So it was a solid mass?*

Erik: It wasn't solid, just super dense space filled with protons and electrons moving around freely. Even now, we can separate protons from electrons without too much trouble.

Maria: We can break atoms apart.

Erik: You can change hydrogen. There are ways to go from one element to another with fusion, fission, or splitting the nuclei. At CERN, we're breaking apart the proton.

Maria: Right, but the nature and the properties of an atom of hydrogen remain the same everywhere. We can manipulate it, break it, or throw it into a supernova star, but its nature remains the same. Its proton doesn't decay. It's completely stable, which is incredible. There are a lot of other radioactive decays, like transmutations, that change particles completely. They decay into two new things that didn't exist inside the original particle, that's quantum mechanics.

Erik: Exactly. If an atom emits a photon, it doesn't mean it's carrying a stash of photons.

Maria: That's how thermonuclear reactions work. One quark becomes another particle plus a neutrino. This is much more than a conventional decay into the components they're composed of. It's a real alchemy of things becoming something completely different.

Erik: The theory is that energy transfers into energy. That's what the old alchemists tried to do with turning lead into gold. Realizing both are energy, they tried to change one energy imprint into another. On the subatomic level, it's a reality today.

AM: *Can we safely harness this as a source of energy, without radioactive waste?*

Erik: There are ways to make energy by changing the particles into different forms of energy, but we don't have a safe way to store it yet.

Maria: That's what nuclear energy is, but you have all the bad junk around it. There's a core group looking into cleaner and less-polluting ideas of cold fusion with inertial confinement and magnetic confinement fusion, but harnessing and controlling those reactions still presents many technical challenges.

AM: *What is the scale of subatomic particles? If you could make an atom the size of a football stadium, what would we see?*

Erik: You can't visualize quantum objects like little balls flying around one another—they're more like waves or ripples on the surface of the ocean. You can't think of them as particles you can localize because in quantum mechanics we're not always certain of where something is even though we can detect it inside an atom or even a nucleus, a proton, or a neutron.

AM: *So they're more like wave forms or energetic events than physical things?*

Erik: They are there, they have a mass, and they're constantly moving.

Maria: They are very much objects of the physical world, but the most powerful electron microscopes only see an atom as a blob and can't image all the particles within it. At the LHC, we see them through their reactions, which allows us to measure their forces and properties.

Erik: We can't see them as tiny balls, but we can track them and mark their movements. We can add up their energies, their charges, and extract from that information their mass. Some of these particles are bound together in the proton and the neutron, but some, like the electron, move around quite freely within the atom.

Maria: They all demonstrate themselves in our experiments. We can measure them as waves and as particles and count the pulse of their charge, if they are charged.

AM: *So like electricity, you can measure their presence, but you can't see them?*

Erik: Essentially, that's right. The image of little balls we're used to is just symbolic, but it's not at all an accurate visual description.

AM: *If everything we see and know equates to just 4 percent of the total energy of the universe, what's the nature of the unseen?*

Erik: That is the big question in physics right now. We've identified and observed the effects of dark energy and dark matter. Of the two, dark energy is the most mysterious. We have no idea how it came to be, but it appears to be everywhere in an equal amount. We see the presence of dark matter through gravitational lensing, the distortion of light from distant galaxies, so it has mass, yet it doesn't attract other things moving around it. Perhaps it's a kind of particle we haven't found yet. It's one of the things scientists are searching for. Maybe it's something about gravity we've yet to understand or about mass that can be described in different ways.

Maria: If the nature of the particles that make everything is quantum, then what is the nature of everything we don't understand? You are targeting the question very well. We think that the nature of dark matter and dark energy has to do with gravity, but we don't have a quantum answer for it yet, and there lies our great dilemma.

Erik: It is one of the big questions in science that we haven't found an answer to yet. There's really not much we know about it. In a way, everything is still possible, and there are many exciting things still to discover.

Maria: I'm currently working on a series of experiments at CERN that I think will reveal the nature of the dark matter as a particle, but Erik doesn't believe it'll be a particle.

Erik: It will not be a particle.

Maria: I'm focusing on it being a particle because in my paradigm, the way I do my experiments, if it is a particle, I will find it. If it is not a particle, I'll have to start from scratch, and my own dream of finding the nature of dark matter is gone.

Erik: All our current research is trying to answer this question, but we honestly don't know the nature of dark matter yet. It's a huge mystery. We really don't understand 96 percent of the universe, but we think that it's around 70 percent dark energy and 26 percent dark matter.

Maria: It's embarrassing!

Erik: Yes, but it makes it such an exciting time because there's still so much to discover.

AM: *Could gravity be a hidden force attracting matter, making the planets, stars, and galaxies, as opposed to matter's own gravitational force being what attracts other matter?*

Erik: This is the way we think matter has ended up in galaxies. First, matter was spread evenly throughout space. Then, gravity did its work and clumped it together. Massive objects are made because gravity pulled them together. Gravity makes these things happen, not the other way around. There are many things we don't yet understand about it. We have to think about space-time and how it curves to understand why it's happening and where the mechanisms behind it come from.

AM: *Is gravity a force beyond space or time?*

Erik: I can understand time without space, but not gravity without space. Gravity and space are completely connected. Without time, you don't have energy, so without space, I don't think you have gravity. Gravity is a very general principle, but it only comes about when space enters the picture. I don't think there was gravity before space.

Maria: If you have space, do you have to have gravity?

Erik: Yes. As soon as you talk about space, you have to talk about the material within it. Gravity is inevitable and universal—it's just there when you don't even assume it could be there.

Maria: That's kind of ridiculous. Why can't you have space alone without gravity?

Erik: Well, that's a mathematical concept. The strength of gravity has to do with the amount of material in a universe. If space is packed full of an infinite amount of material, you can't have gravity, but if you give space a finite amount of material, then you get gravity.

AM: *So did gravity come from the big bang, or was it here before it?*

Erik: The emergence of space has to be correlated with the emergence of gravity, so I don't think it was here before the big bang, at least not as we experience it.

AM: *What do you think was here before?*

Erik: Dark energy, which is happening all the time, and from it dark matter might come. These are just different forms of energy that can go from one thing to another.

AM: *Is dark energy expanding?*

Erik: In our current model of the universe, it is expanding into nothing, and dark energy is the force accelerating that expansion at an ever-increasing rate. However, I don't agree with this model. If dark energy is expanding with the universe, it should be dissipating, but it isn't. It's getting more powerful. That means the energy density of our universe is growing, so its ever-increasing acceleration must be a result of it expanding into and absorbing dark energy.

Maria: What do the cosmologists say? How do they get away from this problem?

Erik: Einstein's equation defines gravity's energy in a very complicated way, which only works in a universe with no time evolution. Many are happy with that, but I'm not. I don't believe the way we think about gravity or the way Einstein wrote it down is correct. However, just as science doesn't want you to ask what was here before the big bang or what our universe is expanding into, it also treats Einstein's equations as unquestionable and unalterable truths.

AM: *You mean they're no longer just a definition, they've become a dogma?*

Maria: They're definitions that have worked very well so far…

Erik: It's a dogma the scientific community is not ready to give up. Yes, it's worked well, but now there are so many questions we can't answer. The problems of dark energy and dark matter are telling us that we need a new way to see and understand beyond Einstein.

AM: *I had no idea we'd already outgrown Einstein or that the universe's accelerating expansion is a result of absorbing the dark energy it's expanding into.*

Erik: In physics we talk about motion, things changing, in an abstract way but not what space is. It's the place where things are changing, but in it there must be many more degrees of freedom than the dimensions we currently know. We see our space expanding as part of a much bigger story. What happened before the big bang could well be something much more mysterious than anything we can visualize or imagine.

AM: *Is the universe a firework that's destined to just burn out, as Lawrence Krauss believes?*

Erik: In Lawrence's model, the universe expands until all the galaxies are eventually drifting in solitary space, and there'll be very little energy left so everything will just taper off. However, I don't agree with that model. I think energy is constant, and the energy that created the big bang was already there. I don't think that we're on a dying firework, but it may be hard to do anything with the 70 percent of dark energy that fills our universe.

Maria: I don't know how to think of the energy of the big bang.

Erik: The current idea isn't well defined, but I believe there has always been energy, and it will still be there as the universe keeps expanding.

Maria: New space-time is constantly being created at the edge of the universe.

Erik: I like to think of our universe as being embedded in a big sea of energy, and that's where the energy of the big bang came from. It must have already been there.

Maria: The standard scientific picture is not like that now. It says that there was nothing and we're expanding into nothing.

Erik: Like a balloon that's being blown up.

Maria: We say it's like a balloon, but then not like a balloon.

Erik: A balloon we can think about as being in our space as a surface, but the universe is described now like the surface of the balloon without the space around it.

AM: *So does that open the concept of a multiverse?*

Erik: I feel that's trying to confine the mystery into something we already know and recognize. Just because it happened here doesn't mean it'll happen the same way out there. If there are different universes, they could have completely different properties. It makes you wonder: Why is our universe like it is? Why do the electrons have the properties they have?

Maria: Everywhere in our universe, it's a universal law.

Erik: They could have been slightly different, which would have given us a totally different universe. So maybe there are universes where things are slightly different, but that's just science fiction. In science, if you can't measure it, it's better not to talk about it.

AM: *Tell us what you've learned about supersymmetry at CERN.*

Maria: Supersymmetry is a beautiful theory that proposes a quantum dimension in which every entity of every particle has a twin, like yin and yang, but we can only see them together in the "super world." The only difference between these twins is the direction of their spin. For every electron, there is a selectron, and when you ride the electron field into the superspace, you part the electron and selectron. We would have found these theoretical twins if their masses were the same, but they aren't, so we started tweaking supersymmetry. Now we call it a broken symmetry because the hidden masses have to be very heavy. None of the current experimental results violate the idea of supersymmetry. On the contrary, they might still give us a dark matter particle, and if dark matter is a particle, we need a theory that connects it to the standard model.

AM: *Is string theory workable?*

Erik: I'm a string theorist. It is not an easy theory. We've learned a lot, but as humans, we're struggling with how to take the next step in answering the big questions. We need a decade or two to make the next big breakthrough. It's on the right track, but I don't know where we're going to end up.

AM: *Finally, have either of you had any personal experiences with things you'd call truly mysterious?*

Erik: There is no bigger mystery than life itself and the fact that this universe exists.

Maria: I'll be more specific. Human intelligence is truly incredible. The level that organized life has risen to, where we're having this discussion, now that's a mystery!

Erik: Mystery also has to do with how we feel as humans and how we react to everything around us. Nothing has happened to me that I could relate to Spirit, but I believe every human has a spirit of some sort. Where it is and where it goes is hard to answer scientifically.

AM: *What an incredible insight you've given us into the depth of our knowledge, and the mystery surrounding it, that science has illuminated. Thank you both so much.*

Chapter 37

Dr Lawrence Krauss

Lawrence Krauss (PhD Massachusetts Institute of Technology & BSc Carleton University) is foundation professor in the School of Earth and Space Exploration and director of the Origins Project at Arizona State University. He is also the author of several bestselling books, including *The Physics of Star Trek*, *A Universe from Nothing*, and *Atom*. In his work as a theoretical physicist and cosmologist, he is a proponent of the idea that the universe is essentially a firework that is destined to finally burn itself out in an ever-accelerating spread trillions of years in the future. He is also a keen advocate of scientific skepticism, science education, and the science of morality. Many of his lectures are available on YouTube, and they are an absolute must-watch. He's a wonderfully entertaining speaker, and any of the great debates on the existence of God that feature him are essential YouTube viewing.

AM: *What is the nature of dark matter and dark energy?*

Lawrence: Of course if we knew the answer to that question, we wouldn't be looking. We've calculated that about 30 percent of the total energy in the universe resides in dark matter because there is more mass than we can account for by all the protons and neutrons in the universe. We're pretty certain that it's an undiscovered type of elementary particle that was created in the early universe. We're searching for it in many different ways, including at the Large Hadron Collider and with direct detection experiments in deep mines underground. Hopefully, we'll discover its nature in the next decade or so.

AM: *There was a recent announcement from the International Space Station saying they found hints of antimatter in their Alpha Magnetic Spectrometer. Does that open the door to a new understanding of dark matter?*

Lawrence: No, it's proof that you should be skeptical of anyone making announcements. Namely, there is a signal, which might be due to dark matter, but it could easily be due to any other number of things, like pulsars. One should be very cautious about claims from those who want to keep funding for some experiment or other. We've been seeing such signals for over a decade, and so far, there has been no evidence that they have anything to do with dark matter. The possibility is exciting, but it's premature to suggest that it's in any way direct evidence of dark matter. In any case, as difficult or exciting as it is to search for dark matter, the stuff that's more important for the future of the universe is dark energy.

Dark energy makes up 70 percent of the universe and without a doubt is the biggest mystery in science. We have no understanding of it whatsoever, and all we can do is detect it indirectly through its influence on the universe. It's mysteriously and completely inexplicable at this point. There are many other things in the universe that we haven't seen yet, like particles called neutrinos. We believe that they formed at the very beginning of time, and we're pretty certain that they're there, but we haven't yet figured out how to detect them. There should also be traces of gravitational waves from the earliest moments of the expansion of the universe, but we don't yet know how to detect those, either. Potentially, there are a host of other mysterious things that we don't yet know exist, so we have to keep looking.

AM: *What was here before the big bang, and what is our universe expanding into?*

Lawrence: First of all, there's no need for our universe to expand into anything, that's a common misconception. Our universe can expand without expanding into anything. It can be all there is. Space can be all there is, and space can get bigger without expanding into anything. A balloon looks like it's expanding into a room when you blow it up, but that's only because you're embedding it in a higher dimensional space. If the surface of the balloon was all there was, the balloon would be getting bigger and wouldn't be expanding into anything, so it's not clear that anything existed before the big bang. It's also possible that there was no before the big bang. Space and time are connected by relativity, so it could be that time itself began at the big bang. Our definition of time is based on our experience and understanding of it within our universe, but it may not have existed before the big bang. We just don't know. Our universe might also be one of an infinite number of universes popping into existence, a multiverse. In that case, there would be time and space outside of our universe, but these are speculative ideas that we may never be able to prove.

AM: *If the energy in the proton has remained essentially the same since the birth of the universe, is that atomic force a direct line to the power of the big bang?*

Lawrence: I wrote a book called *Atom* that tells you that atoms weren't around at the beginning of the universe. They've only existed in their present form since the universe was around four hundred thousand years old, but most of the atoms in our universe haven't been around in their present form that long. The makeup of atoms—the power of the atom, if you wish, is powering the stars. In the process, they're converting hydrogen to helium to carbon to nitrogen to oxygen, and then they explode, spreading those materials through space and eventually arising in our bodies.

AM: *What is the chance that life exists throughout the universe?*

Lawrence: We've discovered evidence of amino acids in comets and organic materials in interstellar space, and there are certainly habitable zones around other stars. We've already discovered planets there, too. That doesn't mean they're inhabited or even habitable, they're just in the zones where liquid water can exist, but there may be other conditions that preclude life. Still, there is every reason to expect that in the hundred billion stars in our galaxy there may be ten billion solar systems similar to ours and maybe a billion planets with habitable zones in which life may arise. If you multiply that by the four hundred billion galaxies we've identified, that is a universe of possibility.

AM: *Those are pretty good odds for life.*

Lawrence: It depends—it may be, or it may be not. Life might require many other things to arise that we don't know about, so it's an open guess at this point. We're lucky that we've been relatively quiescent in our galaxy for the last four or five billion years, and that's what has allowed life to evolve here, apart from the odd meteorite wiping it out periodically.

AM: *What do you think caused the big bang?*

Lawrence: I have no idea, and if I did, I'd publish it! From what I do know, I believe it arose spontaneously from nothing. The laws of quantum gravity would require such an event to happen. It's a random, spontaneous creation caused by the laws of nature, rather like radioactive particles decaying. There's no purpose, no design. It's just an event.

AM: *So the old idea of there being a "big crunch" is irrelevant conjecture?*

Lawrence: Yes, the evidence suggests that the universe will expand forever, as far as we can tell today.

AM: *Have you had any personal experiences with things you'd call really mysterious?*

Lawrence: Well, the universe is mysterious. That's why I do science, to find the mysteries and try to resolve them. It's an exciting, remarkable, and exhilarating program constantly full of surprises. Every day we're discovering new cosmic mysteries that lead to the opening of new windows of understanding.

AM: *How much more is there that we still don't know?*

Lawrence: There's much more about the universe that we don't know than we do. We've only scratched the surface. All of our knowledge, all of our science, is confined to just 4 percent of what's in our universe. Despite our ability to see into the realms of gamma rays, microwaves, ultraviolet, infrared, and the subatomic, we're nowhere near knowing everything. However, it's my belief that nothing is unexplainable, it's just temporarily unexplained.

AM: *Thank you so much for participating in the book.*

* * *

On a personal note, I was surprised that Lawrence, a giant in the world of theoretical cosmology, has a more defined and confined view of the universe than our subatomic physicists, Erik and Maria. The key point is that like them, he clearly says that we only understand a fraction of our reality, but that despite recognizing the extent of the mysterious, he is dogmatically closed minded when it comes to Spirit. Then again, I am certain that I would be too, if it wasn't for the direct experiences I've had that set me off on this voyage of discovery.

Chapter 38

Dr. Maria Spiropulu

After the experiments at the Large Hadron Collider received the Nobel Prize, I arranged a second interview with Maria to ask some follow-up questions about the nature of the fields that permeate the subatomic realm to see if I could find a connection between them and what some of the mediums referred to as the Source or Source Field.

AM: *Congratulations on the Nobel Prize. How did your team get chosen?*

Maria: The Nobel committee never bestows its science prize to teams, so it was given to Mr. Higgs and Mr. Englert, who theorized the existence of the Higgs boson. My team conducted the experiments that proved its existence, so without us, the theorists wouldn't have won the prize, and that's why we celebrate it as all of ours.

AM: *Bravo. I'm so happy for you all. Since our last interview, I've become aware of the concept and importance of fields in the subatomic realm. Could you tell us a bit about them?*

Maria: Quantum field theory describes the interactions of subatomic particles at the quantum level. Instead of talking about quantum forces and quantum particles, we talk about quantum fields. Einstein identified that particles have a duality, being both particles and waves, at the beginning of the twentieth century. He defined this quantum of energy by measuring the particles and the energetic phenomena that binds them, which demonstrates itself in waves, or pulses of electromagnetism. By merging the notions of particles and waves in quantum physics, you arrive at the concept of a field. So the particles and the forces create the field and also fill the field, which means the source of the field and the field acting on the source become interconnected. The phenomena is not separated, and this is why field is a better description.

AM: *So is it possible that the source of the thing is contained within the field?*

Maria: You could say that the source is the generator of the field. In the particles we're studying, their force is turned on by them having a connection with the Higgs field, but the most puzzling question is: what turns on the Higgs field?

AM: *So you're observing the Higgs field as a creative phenomenon?*

Maria: Yes, and this is why people like to refer to it as the "God particle." It creates both the interactions and the masses for the elementary particles, but even more bizarrely, it also creates itself. This self-interaction completely changes the paradigm of our understanding of reality, and measuring how is our new preoccupation.

AM: *So the Higgs field creates itself?*

Maria: Yes, it wouldn't be there if it wasn't turning itself on. If you want to talk about real mystery, this is it.

AM: *In my interviews with the mediums and spiritualists, they constantly used the term Source, or Source Field. Could a field like the Higgs field have been here before the universe, and even given birth to it?*

Maria: I'm not really sure what they're calling Source, but in terms of particles, it's not just the individual particles and their fields that created the universe. There have to have been many, many subsequent interactions to create our observed universe.

AM: *At CERN, do you discuss the concept of the energy that gave birth to the big bang?*

Maria: It's important to remember that the big bang is still just a theory because we only have measurements that describe the universe after the big bang. When it comes to the nature of space-time seen from our point of view from within the universe, we must be careful to recognize the difference between a theory and conjecture. The current proposal of the universe's inflation came about in the 1980s as an answer to a bunch of cosmological puzzles, such as the origin of large-scale structures, and it explains all the measurements we have today. But there could be other explanations. We have yet to figure out where we are in terms of our notions of space-time, and we may have to give up some of the things we like about space-time. This is what string theory attempted, but everything that's been tried to explain space-time is troubling. Space-time has to do with gravity, but we don't have the quantum field of gravity yet, and therein lies the big dilemma of whether gravity is a fundamental force or whether it emerges from something else.

AM: *I feel it must be a fundamental force, almost like a tapestry within the universe. Its ultimate expression is in the black holes, and we don't know what the consequence of those are.*

Maria: That's right. We don't have a good understanding of it yet. We call gravity one of the fundamental forces of nature, but this is also coming to question.

AM: *You mean whether it is an emergent force of creation or a consequential one?*

Maria: We can question whether everything we call fundamental is emergent or consequential, and if you ask this question, then you get yourself into trouble.

AM: *It's a great question though.*

Maria: It is a very good question, yes, and to answer it, we might need to revise, upgrade, or retire some of the ideas we have been using in physics.

AM: *That really underlines the depth of the mystery of everything.*

Maria: Yes, I really think so.

AM: *So despite our current knowledge, this universe is every bit as mysterious as Spirit.*

Maria: Exactly. I like that way of saying it. Everything you've discussed about Spirit is really no more mysterious than the mysteries of our physical realm.

Section Five

The Spiritual Leaders

Chapter 39

An Enlightened Perspective

All religions, all this singing, is one song.
The differences are just illusion and vanity.
Sunlight looks a little different
on this wall than it does on that wall
and a lot different on this other one,
but it is still one light.

Rumi

In this section, I want to share the perspectives of those who've dedicated their lives to service in the name of Spirit and made a daily practice of helping those in need. They don't just talk the talk, they really walk the walk. However, before I do, I wish to explain how I came to choose these three unique individuals.

I lost my religion when I was a kid. I remember the moment clearly, I was sitting in Scripture studies, gazing out the window at the beautiful day, when it hit me. The Creator wouldn't want us in this dusty old classroom, with our noses dug into worn old books. He, or she, would want us outside, playing, singing, dancing, and celebrating the majesty of creation. From that moment on the fanciful tales of kings, carpenters, and shepherds of the distant past became nothing but stories. Long crystalized stories that turn into dogmas, and become anointed as Scriptures. It all seemed like a misunderstanding, of the perfection that is the unfolding of the present.

The prophets of the past may well have had visions, performed miracles, and inspired their followers to form religions. However, the religions that have grown up around them have morphed into massive, multinational corporations that have completely lost sight of the teachings of love and inspiration that gave birth to them. Historically, religion has been the greatest divider of humanity, setting tribe against tribe, country against country, and even brother against brother. But for what?

This is a universe, a single entity. It is one, we are one. None are chosen more than the other. We are all equal. We are all children of creation. And nowhere is creation more apparent than in the present. Our lives are in the here and now. This is the most sacred moment, and in this moment, the best we can do is make the lives of all those around us better. Joy and enjoyment of creation are the greatest prayers, the greatest respects, and the greatest action is in serving others, helping bring them to their joy. That's why I chose those who have dedicated their lives to doing what I see to be truly spiritual work in the present.

One is considered a modern-day saint in India, and he has been on his spiritual path since he was a small child. He always knew it was his destiny to be in service to the light and help his fellow man in every way. The other two are both Jewish Americans who've turned from the faith of their birth to find their own spiritual path within the world's oldest religion.

Chapter 40

His Holiness Swami Chidanand Saraswatiji and Sadhvi Bhagawati Saraswati

His Holiness Swami Chidanand Saraswatiji is the president and spiritual head of the Parmarth Niketan Ashram in Rishikesh, India. It is one of India's largest spiritual institutions. He is also the founder and spiritual head of the Hindu Jain Temple of Pittsburgh. He conceived the idea and laid the foundation for the eleven-volume *Encyclopedia of Hinduism* in 1987.

Sadhvi Bhagawati Saraswati grew up in Los Angeles and attended Stanford University before going to India when she was twenty-five. What started as a short trip turned into a new life studying and living in seva (as a student in divine service) to His Holiness Swami Chidanand Saraswatiji.

AM: *How is Spirit bound to matter, giving us the experience of life?*

Sadhvi Bhagawati: When we talk about Spirit and matter, most of us think of them as separate. So, for example, the material perspective, the perspective based on matter, says: This is who I am. This is me. I end here. And then we have space. You begin here. You end on that other side of you. That's the world of matter. In the world of Spirit, there is no distinction. The Spirit that flows through me is the same Spirit that flows through you. There is no place where I end and you begin. There is no empty space between us, it is all Spirit. The core concept of spirituality is that rather than being focused on this flesh, this empty space, that person, and that empty space, we focus on the Spirit that flows between. And yet, as beautiful as it is to discuss spirituality in that way, we can take it a step deeper. It's really important to understand that everything has Spirit in it. If you're going to ask the question of how Spirit is bound to matter, you're already implying that they're two separate things united in some agreeable way, but I would suggest that it's all Spirit. We have different vehicles for it, different vessels of it, different reflections of it, and different manifestations of it, regardless of whether we think of it as living or inanimate.

I once asked a religious teacher who is considered a saint in India about the different manifestations of the divine. My question was that if Lakshmi is the divineness of wealth, Ganesh is the remover of obstacles, and Saraswati is the divineness of knowledge and music, what if you mess up and pray to the wrong one at the wrong time? What if you ask Lakshmi for wisdom, or you ask Sirish Swathi to remove your obstacles?

He is known to be a very strict adherent to the book, so his answer surprised me. He picked up a little table and said, "You could pray to this, and if your prayer was sincere and your heart was sincere and it was meant to happen, your prayer will be answered." I say this because the table is clearly matter, on a scale of Spirit to matter, it's way over toward matter. Here is one of the wisest teachers, highest in the hierarchy of the carriers of wisdom in India, picking up a table and saying that to which we pray in a temple is here in the table. So when we talk about the Spirit being bound to matter, I'd say matter is infused with Spirit. The fact that the table is not aware that the Spirit is in it, in the same way that you are aware of the Spirit in you, doesn't mean it is any less there. So when we talk about giving us the experience of life, that's where consciousness comes in. The table may or may not be aware of the Spirit in it, and it may or may not be conscious of having a life, but we are.

AM: *So consciousness is the answer?*

His Holiness Swami Chidanand Saraswatiji: Consciousness is the answer, consciousness of the Spirit. In India, when we meet, we greet by saying "Namaste." There is a message in that Namaste, and there is an answer to your question in that Namaste. It literally means "I see the divine in you." When you start living on that level, seeing the divine in everyone and everything, then life changes, immediately. That Namaste changes the whole spectrum of your life. When you start seeing Spirit in all, the same divine in all, the name of the divine doesn't matter. When you start living on that level, my dear, you will see the difference. Living on this level, there is no give and take, it is only give, give, give. The way you want to be loved and the way you want to be held, you want to do unto others. It is not a question of matter or Spirit, but how we live by that Spirit in divine consciousness every minute and every moment. That is how you start living on the level of pure consciousness: treating others as you want to be treated. The Spirit of the other is the same Spirit as you, so if you don't want to be deceived, don't deceive. If you don't want to be hurt, don't hurt. Or if you don't want to be cheated, don't cheat. See? The same divinity in all. With that beginning, life changes. It becomes so beautiful, so peaceful, so meaningful. Spirit is just waiting to make you free.

AM: *Is destiny a script we can't deviate from, or are we free to alter our destiny?*

Sadhvi Bhagawati: The answer is both. That which you have today, which is your destiny for today, is unaltered. If I planted peach seeds last year, I'm going to have a peach tree this year. It doesn't matter how many apple mantras, apple prayers, apple songs, apple vision sessions, or apple mediations I do, there is no way I'm going to get an apple tree to grow out of that peach seed. The best I'm going to get is a peach tree. It can't be altered. I can't go back and plant an apple seed so that today I can have apples. So now I have peaches when I really want apples, but I'm stuck. I can't change what I planted, I can only reap what I sowed, and that is where most of our depression and frustration comes from. We waste time, energy, and even lives bemoaning the fact that we have peaches and not apples. No matter how many apple prayers we do, those aren't the actions to get what we want.

Today what is in your hand is written, but it was written based on what you've done. The stars didn't say, 'This man shall have peaches'. You planted a peach seed. The law of nature did the rest, and that's why you have peaches, but tomorrow is not written. It is not written that you shall have peaches forever. If you want apples, go out and plant an apple seed, water it, and let the sun shine on it, and you'll get apples next year.

We can't redo the school we went to, the parents we had, or choices we made over the last however many years of life. We can't reauthor where we are today, but with acceptance, we can change tomorrow. That is where free will comes in, but the challenge is that no matter how much we read, hear, and intuit, we keep doing the thing that gives us the old outcome because it's familiar, it's what we know. Changing your destiny is about changing your patterns. It takes the power of discrimination to say, 'Wait, how much of this is habit? Is this based on choices I am making? How much of this can I change?' It's in that awareness that we start to alter our lives.

AM: *Karma, how does it work? Does it affect Spirit? Do we carry it through many lifetimes, and is it changeable?*

His Holiness Swami Chidanand Saraswatiji: The whole philosophy of spirituality is how to become free from karma because we are the fruit of karma. Whatever you do now, you see tomorrow and in the future. So if I am experiencing the fruits of karma, the consequences of my actions, it means firstly, I have to become aware that I am the reason, and secondly, I must use this awareness to make me aware that I can free myself of this karma.

We all have to perform karma if we're here on this earth. No one escapes without performing the karma. Every action you take generates karma, and that becomes your destiny and your life. Now, how to become free? In the scripture, there is a beautiful mantra given when this question is raised and the answer is given. By focusing on this mantra and making it a conscious prayer coming from the depths of your heart, you can change your karma: "Oh Lord, whatever karma, whatever actions I have performed through my body, my senses, my mind, my intellect, and my nature, all of that, Oh Lord, I lay at your holy feet. Not only my actions, but the fruit of those actions, too, I lay at your holy feet. Even my thoughts, as they create karma, I lay these at your holy feet, too."

It means whatever is done and is thought is being given to the divine. It is part of you, and you are part of the divine. They say when you perform the karma, if you become free from the doership, it means you become the instrument, the tool. I am merely a tool that the divine's grace has given me, and I will use this tool to serve. Then the karma, that action you are trying to undo the consequence of, will not limit you or bind you because you are not the doer, the divine is. You are just the divine's tool. Whatever you do, offer to the divine. Become the tool, the instrument of the divine, and then the karma you are performing will never bind you. This is how to be free from the karma.

Think of an accountant working for a company. The money comes and goes, and he enters it all in the computer. Regardless of whatever the profit and loss of the company is, he goes home and sleeps easy. The owner of the company may be tossing and turning in his bed if there is a loss, but not the accountant. He knows he is just the accountant, and whatever happens around him is not his fault. He gives the accounts to the owner. Well, this is the same thing. Be like the accountant, and give all of that to the owner of the world, and let the owner carry that burden. It's his world. We're just his instruments. Look at the sunset, the sunrise, the stars, and the moon. They are always on time. They're never even a fraction of a second late. Everything's always running in such a beautiful way, but we keep worrying about the smallest of issues. Why?

The answer is to become the instrument and live in total consciousness. We will always generate karmas. We are not saints. We are human. But when you live in that consciousness, that awareness, karma will never bind you, limit you, or shackle you. You will become free, and this is the secret of living a divine life, a beautiful life.

AM: *You've just given us a wonderful key to lighten our spiritual burdens in this incarnation. Thank you.*

Chapter 41

Radhanath Swami

Radhanath Swami is a Hare Krishna guru and spiritual teacher of bhakti yoga. Born Richard Slavin in suburban Chicago, he's devoted his life to the search for a greater spiritual truth. At thirty-one, he took the monastic vows of Vaishna, which is when he became known as Radhanath Swami. Today, he lives mostly at the Radha Gopinath Temple in Chowpatty, Mumbai, but travels regularly throughout India, Europe, and North America sharing the teachings of bhakti yoga. For the past twenty-five years, he's guided the Krishna community's development and directed social projects such as Midday Meals, which daily serves more than 260,000 plates of sanctified, vegetarian food to the children who live in the slums of Mumbai. He's also worked to establish missionary hospitals, eye camps, eco-friendly farms, schools, ashrams, an orphanage, and a number of emergency-relief programs throughout India. A few years ago, he also completed the story of his own spiritual journey in his autobiography, The Journey Home.

AM: *How did your journey into Spirit begin?*

Radhanath Swami: As a child, the contradictions I saw made in the name of religion greatly disturbed me. There was so much hate and war, all in the name of a supposedly loving God. Breaking into my teens, I started seeing both sides of the coin. On one hand, religion is a terribly divisive and destructive force in our world, but on the other, there's something beautiful and loving entwined within its teachings. I decided to make finding and understanding that spiritual core, the pure essence within each religion, my goal. Over the next several years, I studied many different religious systems, and then when I got into my twenties, I decided to travel abroad to see how people viewed God and morals and what makes life really worthwhile outside of America. During that trip, a yearning—a calling—awoke inside me, pulling me toward something spiritual. I went to several monasteries, trying to discover what it was when one day, out of the blue, I just knew inside that I had to go to India. I hitchhiked from London to the Himalayas, studying Judaism, Christianity, and Islam along the way. Then arriving in India, I immersed myself in various sects of Hinduism and Buddhism. That's when the essential common thread in all these great spiritual traditions really became apparent, as did the prison of fundamentalism that exists within every religion. It made me realize that the rigid adherence to dogma is one of humanity's greatest failings, and yet it exists in every walk of life, from science to religion and everything in between. This rejection of the new, or what doesn't fit with some preconceived convention, is an inflexibility centered in the ego, and unless we can put that ego aside, we can never find the beauty we all have in common. That is the harmony that transforms lives, brings hope, peace, and inner fulfillment. Once that connection is made, we begin to understand and experience others with love and really connect to one another from within. In that empathic love, we cannot hate anyone. I've given my life into going deeper and deeper into that experience and trying to share it with others.

AM: *Was there a moment of realization that brought you to where you are now?*

Radhanath Swami: Yes, but there was a quick succession leading up to it. I'd just returned to London from the Isle of Wight Festival, where I saw Jimi Hendrix play his final UK show. His sudden death a few weeks later really affected me as I was far from home and searching for the answers of life. When this incredible talent, this bright light, was suddenly snuffed out, I realized that you can have everything, talent, fame, money, and so much opportunity, yet still be unhappy and unfulfilled. Every evening after he died, I'd go and sit on the Thames Embankment and gaze at the Thames rolling by, wondering where the river of destiny was leading me and where I really wanted to go. One day walking back to where I was staying, I spontaneously popped into a church, sat, and opened a Bible. The first passage my eyes settled on the line that read *come out from among them, and be ye separate.* Right after that, I packed up and started wandering. First, I went to see the cathedrals of Italy, and then I went to the island of Crete, where I ended up living in a cave on the south coast practicing my meditation. It was there that I heard a voice in my heart say, "Go to India." That was when all of this really began in earnest.

AM: *I'd like to ask you some questions that I've asked the other interviewees to get your perspective. How is Spirit bound to matter, giving us this life experience?*

Radhanath Swami: What I've learned through my teachers, my experiences in life, and the scriptures I've studied is that there is energy, and there is energetic. Spirit is the energetic, the Source, and matter is the manifestation of that energy. In our bodies, Spirit is the living force that sees, hears, tastes, smells, thinks, and loves. Spirit activates, witnesses, and experiences life through our bodies. The body is an instrument for Spirit to experience life, and how we do so is a reflection of our individual state of consciousness. Of course, we can lift our state of consciousness by harmonizing with Spirit through meditation, yoga, prayer, song, laughter, joy, and creation.

All the species of life throughout our universe share Spirit because it's the source of life. It creates, sustains, energizes, and activates. You can see it and feel it in nature. Science is the study of that energy, and it's incredible how much has been discovered about it on both the micro and the macro levels. Spirituality is the alignment with the force of Spirit that creates, energizes, and activates physical energy. In the past, when scientists started to analyze and understand the nature of matter, the incredible discoveries they made flew in the face of religion. If what they said wasn't spoken about in the scriptures, it was considered heresy, which meant they'd often be persecuted, prosecuted, or worse for peeling back the blinders of ignorance. The conservative fundamentalists who've always held religion in a viselike grip would say if it wasn't written in their holy book, then it was blasphemy. Today, the tables are somewhat turned, as science has become the religion of the unreligious and itself is full of fundamentalists who decry religion. Of course, to make things worse, the world is still full of fundamentalist religious zealots who decry material science and everything else that isn't in their holy book. Until we break down these walls and open ourselves to understand the possibilities and prophecies of one another's paths, we have no hope of freeing ourselves from the divisiveness of dogma and those using it to empower themselves.

AM: *What do you think binds the subatomic particles together to create matter?*

Radhanath Swami: From a spiritual perspective, I believe there's some kind of intelligence entwined in the fabric of our universe that is both transcendent and imminent. Through that divine intelligence, matter operates in the most incredible and miraculous ways. Some of us choose to connect to that Spirit, living in its love and grace, while others dive deeply into matter, the what-is, searching for the answers to the mystery of existence in the intricacies of its workings. I feel the truth is in both, and as children of the universe, we must open our hearts to one another to experience a full understanding of all this.

AM: *What is karma, and how does it work?*

Radhanath Swami: Karma is a simple law of nature that says for every action there is a reaction, so as human beings we must be responsible for our actions, our words, and our thoughts. Exactly how, why, and when those reactions come is beyond our understanding, but they can be greatly influenced by the things we've been conditioned to throughout our life. The different experiences we go through in life are responses to or reactions from our previous karmic activities. For example, if you smoke too much, it's very difficult to stop smoking, but if a person has never smoked, not smoking is easy. We condition ourselves to particular realities that dictate our lives, and then karma subjects us to experiences that challenge us to break free and find our own true transcendental identities.

I believe we're all a part of Spirit, the Source. We're used to calling it God, but Spirit has many names in all the different traditions throughout history, and through them **all, you can** have the same genuine experience of transformation. The core of all the spiritual teachings is the realization that Spirit is eternal and limitless and that we are all a part of it. In my tradition, we call that spirit Krishna, which means the all attractive. Our belief is that love, universal, intimate, ecstatic love, is within us, and we can be instruments of that love in whatever we do and wherever we are. True spiritual practice isn't to be a Jew, a sheikh, a Muslim, a Zoroastrian, or whatever, but rather to connect to the spiritual essence within us and experience the love that is our greatest potential.

AM: *Great answer. Is destiny a script from which we cannot deviate, or can we alter our destiny? Do we come into this life with soul lessons to learn?*

Radhanath Swami: It's both. Let me explain. A week ago, I took British Airways from Mumbai to London. I had free will of both where I wanted to go, and which airline to take, but on the day of departure, my destiny was set. Once the plane took off, I couldn't say I want to go to Singapore instead. The flight attendant would let me know London was my destiny and my destination. So, I had free will, but once I got on the plane, my free will was gone. If you jump off a cliff, you've made that choice, and you don't have much free will as to where you're going. You're destined to hit the ground. The choices you made previously created that destiny.

Free will is the most precious and powerful thing in making our destiny. Once we do something, we have no choice as to what the reaction is going to be. But even if the reaction is negative, we can still turn it around by doing positive things, and that will generate positive reactions. Whatever comes to us, we have the free will of how we're going to respond to it. So in that sense, what we're experiencing now is destiny. There is a script, one we've already chosen. We don't decide we want to suffer, but if we do something that creates negative karma, then we've written the script. It'll come back around to us to deal with again, but then we're free to choose how we respond to each of those situations, and that determines our future destiny. Free will is never taken away from us.

Let's take the eternality of the soul. I've been in monasteries where the monks of the Christian faith believe in reincarnation and the eternality of the soul in life after life. It's at the core of Buddhism and Hinduism as well as many other faiths. So our souls picked our destinies, choosing these lives we're each in, just like getting on that airplane. We bring karma from our previous lives as well as having the karma we create in this life, but seen from the eternal perspective of the soul, our free will has the transformation potential in all situations. You can get on that plane and make everyone around you happy, make them laugh, and let your kindness comfort their journey, or you can argue, fight, and sulk all the way, and then everyone on the plane will hate you by the time you arrive. That's where free will comes in, allowing you to control your karma, and thus, influence your destiny.

AM: *What do you wish for humanity?*

Radhanath Swami: I hope the incredible progress in technology and science comes together with spirituality. I see spirituality as being about character and compassion. As we have seen in the past, if technology is not used with compassion, it can create ecological and environmental disasters. It can also be used to construct an Orwellian state and allow for people like Hitler to rise again. He was surrounded by fantastic scientists creating missiles, bombs, planes, tanks, and all the other extraordinary tools of destruction. Humanity needs to cultivate an ethical, moral, and compassionate consciousness to keep these great technologies we're developing in check and make sure that they live up to their potential of benefitting the world, not destroying it.

We're all connected, so unless we recognize the sacredness of our own lives and the Spirit within us, we won't be able to recognize the sacredness of the Spirit within others. If we only see our differences, such as "I'm white, and they're black," "I'm Hindu, and they're Muslim," or "I'm male, and they're female," we're just seeing the external, material designations but not what we're all connected to. I don't mean just lip service to understanding, but a real inner realization that we're all related, we're made of the same substance, and we're from the same origin. We are all brothers and sisters. If you really love yourself, you will naturally love the self within others and see the common Spirit within us all. That is what I hope for the world.

AM: *Beautiful. I hope we see this transformation in our lifetimes.*

Section Six

Lost at Sea in an Endless Mystery

Chapter 42

In Closing

We've experienced Spirit through real life stories and heard from psychics, seers, scientists, and spiritual leaders. What resonates through all of this is the depth of the mystery that surrounds us. This book started out with my own quest to know more, but I realize it's impossible to find all the answers. If you go into the greatest library in the world, you'll never be able to read all the books, and if you try, you'll miss out on life completely.

The first section of the book showed us that Spirit can reach across the divide and really make our lives better. The world of Spirit is like a reflection in a mirror: the closer you move toward it, the closer it comes to you. It's there for all of us, especially if we work with really good mediums to help us commune with those on the other side.

In the second section we met our panel of experts, bonafide mediums with a real connection to the other side, who introduced themselves and their process.

In the third section the mediums shared their insights through Spirit, and gave us a glimpse of a possible new understanding of where we really come from and return to. From doing the interviews here and attending the various events since, I believe their gift is a much needed key to change our world. Imagine if this new level of sensitivity was taught and expanded on? It would transform humanity and might even make life on earth heavenly. However all we've learned so far is just that, today's knowledge, but tomorrow our knowledge will grow. There is so much more to be understood about, and from, the realm of Spirit.

In the fourth section, our scientists gave us a clear overview of what we currently know of reality on both the cosmological and the subatomic scales. They impressed me deeply by so freely admitting that all we know is just a fraction of all **there is in our** universe. They all had different degrees of difficulty with the idea of Spirit because they haven't experienced it themselves, and of course, they can't measure it scientifically. Lawrence Krauss, an extraordinarily accomplished professor, totally rejects the possibility of it, standing shoulder to shoulder with the likes of Christopher Hitchens, Richard Dawkins, Bill Nye, and Sam Harris in the great debates against religion and the existence of God. To be honest I'd most likely be with them too, if it wasn't for my own experiences with Spirit.

In the West, we're losing our religion at around the same time in the arc of our history as Rome when it dropped the pantheon of pagan gods for Christ. Their religion failed them, but let's take a moment to look back at polytheism. In our jealous and judgmental brand of monotheism, any kind of fun is considered a sin, but in the polytheistic world you'd have a god for that. Your revelry would be a celebration to Bacchus, the god of partying. In war, you'd pray to Mars or Apollo, and in love, to Diana or Aphrodite. For every occasion and time of life, there was a divinity to turn to and, more importantly, to turn what you were doing into a divine experience. What have the confines of monotheism brought us? A jealous and judgmental god cemented in dogma, inflicting punishment, pestilence, shame, war and inquisition.

The roots of Judaism, Christianity, and Islam can be traced back to Egypt's Aten through Moses. Aten became the sole deity of Egyptian state religion around 1340 BCE during the reign of, and at the order of, Amenhotep IV. He fancied himself as the one and only god's son, so as pharaoh he decreed that there was only one god: his god, Aten. Thus, the first monotheistic religion was born of one man's ego. This was the spiritual reality that Moses grew up under. It was the principal religious influence of his day, so it isn't surprising that on seeing a burning bush, he understood his vision of Spirit to be a visit from a singular deity.

What has our three-plus millennia of worshipping this vengeful, jealous, all-powerful, all-seeing, and patriarchal deity brought us? War, vengeance, divisiveness, hatred, and not a single monument as remarkable as the majestic Pyramids of Giza. They were built over a thousand years before Moses and Amenhotep IV to honor the god Osiris and his goddess, Isis, the principal deities in the first dynasty of Egypt's earlier polytheistic religion.

While it's tempting to cast out our contemporary religions with all their sordid scandals and economic intrigues, we still need spiritual guidance, transformation, love, and hope. In the fifth section, some spiritual leaders of the Hindu faith, the most prominent remaining polytheistic religion, gave some words of gentleness. They inspire us to live life consciously and avoid the boomerang of karma with awareness, mindfulness, and reverence, much as every sage and prophet has done through the ages. Alas, we're human, so righteousness, like diet and exercise, is a great goal but difficult to maintain, especially in our Western lives.

So what's the take-away from all of this?

Spirit is one and many. It will always come to us in a way we'll recognize. It never seeks to frighten and brings only messages of love, guidance, and inspiration. It is of the light because it is light. Those who've passed over say that they experienced death as a rebirth, a coming home, and a reunion. They rejoin their soul family, where they learn from the lessons of this life and prepare to reincarnate. If they've completed their soul-cycle incarnations, then they move up to a place of no fragments, eventually uniting with the Source and enriching and empowering it. From the evidence gathered here, our soul, our Spirit, is a part of the same single Source. That Source has the ability to split itself into many self-aware fragments, and as those fragments fragment, they become us, our many individual souls.

Our planet needs a new story, one that unites humanity as one, and I believe the only place that can come from is Spirit. Now it's time for you to ask your questions, find your own truth, live it, and breathe it. Learn meditation, yoga, and tai chi. Be mindful of your actions, and watch your karma. Remember that prayer is song to Spirit, and music is magic, so practice and enjoy them because they are celebrations of creation. Find or build communities of like-minded people, and refuse to be separated by modern life. We're all surfers riding the waves of energy that is life. We're all Spirit bound to matter and an inseparable part of the Creator experiencing the created. Don't follow someone else's story, create your own, and take an active role in unraveling the mystery of Spirit and what lies beyond.

Special Thanks to:
Jennifer Carno, for all the wonderful transcribing.
Lee Papa, for her excellent editing.
Tom Wszalek, for his connections and encouragement.
John Pearson, for his tireless championing of my writing.
And to everyone who gave their time and shared their stories.
Missy at CreateSpace for a stellar job on the proof read.
Joanna Hadfield for her diligent final edit.

Section Seven

ADDENDUM

Children, Spirit and The Gift

During the interviews I thought it prudent to add a couple of questions to each of our mediums about kids with the gift. I did this in part because for many of them it was a burden, or something that alienated them in childhood, but also because there are so many children being born with the gift, or with a far higher level of sensitivity than those who came before them.

This section is for both parents and children dealing with the gift today.

AM: *How should parents treat children who have these abilities?*

Carissa Schumacher: Parents tend to push their children into certain molds, projecting their beliefs, wishes, and expectations onto them. This restricts their ability to evolve into who they really are, and it also precludes the parents from evolving on their own path to higher consciousness. Today, more than ever, children are being born with a strong sense of intuition and inner knowing. Never before have so many old souls been reborn, which is why so many kids are so much more spiritually advanced than their elders. Of course, this can lead to issues with authority as well as all the distractions they have to contend with, from competition in school to a sea of new technologies. They're wrestling with a level of intuition and sensitivity that those who came before them did not experience. They're able to perceive the world around them on a soul level in ways most of the older generation can't grasp, yet they don't know how to quiet the constant static, the distractions of life, to hear their inner voices and achieve a real awareness of their true selves.

If children say they hear Spirit, or have phobias, or trouble concentrating in school, never be dismissive or say there's something wrong with them. When they speak about their dreams and intuitions, or asks questions about esoteric truths such as death and sexuality, really listen to their questions and ask about what they perceive. If you earn children's trust with unconditional love and respect, they'll be more likely to accept this intuitive part of themselves instead of struggling. If you make them fear or suppress their abilities, it'll lead to bottled-up, emotional explosions, or even severe depression. Set them free to use their imagination, even if you don't understand it. Remember—just because you can't perceive something doesn't mean it isn't real.

Encourage children to be in nature, to draw pictures and write poems of what they perceive. Share stories with them from different cultures so they're free to create their own beliefs instead of imposing yours on them. This will allow both their and your consciousnesses to expand. Work on your own intuitive abilities. Meditate. The further you advance in your enlightenment, the more you'll understand about your intuitive child. Intuition and the ability to see beyond the veils is an extraordinary gift to be nourished and supported, not shoved into a closet. Just because a child is intuitive doesn't mean he'll become a medium, so don't project stereotypes on what it means to be intuitive. The more you empower your child, the easier it'll be for her to come to peace with who she is and to use her abilities in unique and functional ways.

Balanced parenting is essential for raising intuitive children. Love and compassion is essential, but it's equally important to know how to enforce discipline when they act up because they're wise beyond school smarts. You always need to be ten steps ahead of them because without proper boundaries they'll quickly learn how to manipulate the world around them. Most of all, allow them to be children, and never project your own dreams and expectations onto them. Let them BE because they can teach you as much as you can teach them.

AM: *What advice would you give children with these abilities?*

Carissa: There's a reason for every ability you're born with. Your higher self designed the blueprint for your life, so if you incarnated with an ability or gift, it's part of your soul purpose. Never try to tune out your ability because someone tells you what you're feeling isn't real. Trust and respect your abilities by keeping a journal of your experiences, dreams, visions, and sensations. With the help and guidance of your parents, seek out good online resources to learn about others who are experiencing similar things.

Being sensitive and intuitive requires a real awareness of your own needs, so you must practice quality self-care. Learn to meditate, and set boundaries. Your abilities can't be turned off, but by simply breathing and firmly stating your boundaries to yourself, you can set your limits for the communication with Spirit. Learn to create a safe zone where you can retreat so they don't overwhelm you. Remember that the ability to see beyond the veils is a blessing and a gift, so treat it with respect. Most of all, don't allow your ego to claim it, this isn't a superpower to make you superior, but a gift to serve and help others.

Hollister Rand

AM: *What advice would you give parents whose children have these abilities?*

Hollister: Honestly, I always opt for educating the parents first. Acceptance is vital—don't make your child feel strange. However, safety is also very important. You don't want your child inviting a whole world of spirits into your house. Get help from a medium you know and trust so you can teach your child how to set boundaries. Creating your own sanctuary is very important. It really helps if the parents are open and educated when it comes to having a sensitive child.

AM: *What advice would you give children with these abilities?*

Hollister: The first and most important thing to understand is that we can set boundaries for this work and not have your life be high-jacked by spirits whenever they want your attention. As a child, it seemed like I had no control over who was going to show up or when. I'd turn around, and there they were. Or I'd wake up in the middle of the night, and there they were. When you're really open, they're so ever present that it can be overwhelming. There came a time when I was almost feeling victimized by them because I couldn't get any time for myself. Now I work very specifically at the frequency of love and setting clear boundaries. I protect myself, the people around me, and my home with high levels of energy. I've also developed a strong bond with my guides, who are also my psychic protectors.

AM: *Do you have any tips for setting boundaries?*

Hollister: Again, I'd instruct the parents first. Usually if spirits are showing up, there's been some level of an invitation. Of course, there are many different types of spirits: those who are welcomed like family who've passed and imaginary friends who can often be soul companions. Those are usually very comfy visitations, but then there are those who aren't so nice. There are some lost or angry souls stuck here, so it's important to determine who you want in your life and who you don't, just like on the earth plane. Imagine if the playground bully chose to show up every night. That can happen to kids, and it happened to me. As a young spirit who was haunting a client's house once said, "Dying doesn't make you nice!" They're the ones for which a line needs to be drawn. I always tell parents that if there's unwanted attention, then they need to shift the vibration or frequency in their house. Divine love, holy water, sage—there are many ways to do it, and in my book, I lay out several protection exercises.

Thomas John

AM: *How should parents treat children who have these abilities?*

Thomas: Like anything else that makes a kid different, like being gay, it's something parents have to embrace and support. The most important thing is to make kids feel supported, safe, and secure at home because they're going to have a tough time at school. It's completely natural, and it should be encouraged, so I'd suggest finding a teacher or mentor to help them develop and control their gift.

It was a different time when I was growing up twenty-five years ago. There weren't people like Sylvia Browne, John Edward, or Theresa Caputo on TV or in the papers every day, so my parents didn't have any frame of reference to deal with it. Nobody in my family had the gift, so I really was the odd one out. They reacted in a more fear-based way than was ideal, but they realize it now, especially my mom. She's so accepting of things now, but when I was little, she'd make me go to therapists and stuff like that. It made me feel like I was different in a really bad way, and honestly, it wasn't the right way of handling it.

AM: *What advice would you give to children with these abilities?*

Thomas: Surround yourself with like-minded people. Choose your friends carefully at school. Only let those who accept, embrace, and understand your gift become friends. You're going to be much more sensitive to things going on around you than other kids, so it's also very important to learn how to protect yourself by creating boundaries and safe spaces. Psychics, intuitives, clairvoyants, and mediums are more susceptible to things like depression and anxiety because of this. When you see Theresa Caputo on TV with her big blonde wig and long nails, it seems like this is a fun, campy, and cool thing, but it comes with a great deal of responsibility.

It's neither easy nor fun when people are constantly projecting their pain, sadness, longing, and grief on you, hoping you hold the key to their relief or release. If you do decide to tap into it either professionally or just to read your friends, you have to do it with the understanding that it's something you must treat in a special, sacred way.

Lisa Williams

AM: *With your experience, what advice do you have for parents of gifted kids?*

Lisa: First, parents should really listen. Hear and understand what children are saying because they're telling you their truth, and they need to be treated with absolute love and respect. Regardless of whether you think it's just an overactive imagination, you have to be 110 percent supportive. Ask as many questions as you like, respectfully and positively. Ask what they're seeing, sensing, and hearing to understand their gift and those they're dealing with. Don't forget, you are their lifeline to unconditional love and safety. It is your responsibility to help them navigate a world you cannot see, so accept you have as much to learn from them as they do from you.

AM: *What advice would you give kids with the gift?*

Lisa: A lot of kids are scared of it, so the first thing to make them understand is that it's normal and certainly nothing to be scared of. Enjoy it! It's a gift, and know you're not alone. There are many others like you. I tell my son it's fine to talk to them, but I have him keep a journal to record what he hears, sees, and feels. That really helps get a handle on it. Keep things in perspective, and know where you want the boundaries to be.

AM: *So your son has the gift?*

Lisa: Definitely. He's a very spiritual and gifted child. He sees things and is very intuitive. Already, he communicates with the other side constantly, and he has very healing hands. So he has a lot to work with, if he chooses to follow this path.

Jeffrey Wands

AM: *How should parents treat children with these abilities?*

Jeffrey: I'd say just accept it, and don't make a big thing about it. People are more open to it now, but when I was growing up, it was taboo. They'd have thought you were crazy or something was wrong with you.

The important thing is: make sure they know that there's nothing wrong with it, but help them understand that there's a real responsibility that comes with it.

AM: *What advice would you give kids who discover they have the gift?*

Jeffrey: Don't be afraid of it, but understand that with this gift comes great responsibility. You have to learn that you can't just walk up to somebody and give them information just because you have it. You must understand the responsibility of your gift, when it should and shouldn't be used and how it can help, heal.

Demi of California Psychics

AM: *How should parents treat children with these abilities?*

Demi: First and foremost, they must put fear aside and realize this is a divine blessing and a gift. They've been given this to help teach their parents and the planet a new level of awareness. The parents must help them find a support system that doesn't impose any kind of religious structure on them, that's really important. Encourage your kids to talk freely about what they're seeing and hearing, and never judge what you don't understand. Accept it for what it is: their reality. It's very important to remember that being negative creates fear and self-destructive patterns because kids don't know what to do with that information or emotion. You must give them a strong support system so they don't go down that road. From what I've been seeing in our community here in Florida over the last two generations, the gift is getting ever more prevalent. More and more people have the gift. It's as if humanity is moving toward some kind of shift."

AM: *What advice do you have for children with these abilities?*

Demi: I work a lot with mentoring kids privately, and the first thing I like to tell them to do is develop a journal to record their impressions. What are you experiencing? Is it a screen that shows a picture, or a feeling, a sensation, a temperature change, a smell? Keeping track of it will help you identify it and recognize your most prevalent and useful gifts. Build up an understanding of them as tools in a tool box. We all have many of them, but keeping a journal really helps you understand when the gift shows up and to validate its presence. If you get a feeling about someone or something, write it down, regardless of whether it seems right or wrong in the moment. Respect the feeling, and keep revisiting it until you understand the wisdom contained in it.

Ask your parents and/or mentors to work with you to explore your experiences. There are all kinds of spirits on the other side, so finding and recognizing the ones who come in love is important. As you learn to identify which feelings are accurate and coming from a good place, you'll develop your self-esteem and validate that your gift can really help your community. This is the greatest purpose of the gift, to be in service.

Eden of California Psychics

AM: *How should parents treat children with these abilities?*

Eden: I've done a fair bit of parent counseling for this, and the first thing I emphasize is don't put your own personal religious belief system into the equation. Treat it as if your child has a musical or mechanical skill that has to be developed. Don't try to impose any doctrine on it. They need to understand that what they're experiencing is psychic energy without being made to feel bad about it, so don't treat them as different or set them apart. When I tried to suppress my psychic energy as a child, I developed panic attacks, but I didn't have a clue what I was going through because they didn't have a name for panic attacks back then. Psychic energy can manifest itself in the body in many different ways: headaches, ringing in the ears, etc. If your child's been checked by a doctor and there aren't any medical issues cropping up, your child may simply be experiencing psychic energy.

Pay attention to their dreams, and listen to their fears, regardless of whether it's a monster in the cupboard or a beast under the bed because those experiences can really affect them. I know—I slept with the covers over my head until adolescence. Teach them this is all just another facet of their divine essence, of who they are. It's not as hard now as it was in my childhood. There's a lot more written about it. Find reputable people to teach you how to help your kids deal with their abilities. They can often have very bad dreams, and depending on what kind of gifts they have, they may be picking up feelings or energies from others around them. If they're very empathic, this can have a very strong impact on them, so you really need to teach them how to deal with this psychic energy, or find someone who can if you can't.

AM: *What advice do you have for children discovering this within themselves?*

Eden: Like anything else in life, educating yourself is a huge start. With your parents' help, seek out places to discuss these things **with others your** age. Connect with like-minded individuals who have similar gifts, it's much easier now with the Internet. Know it's just another aspect of life. Some kids are great at piano, some at sports. This is your gift, so embrace it.

James of California Psychics

AM: *How should parents treat children with these abilities?*

James: Spirits are so drawn to the innocent light of children on this earth plane. So many people ask me about their two and three year olds who are talking to someone. I always tell them that it's nothing to be frightened of, that it isn't harmful. Children before school age are naturally closer to Spirit because they're so much purer. They just draw it close to them, but it's only coming forward in love. In my experience, as children start school, Spirit will take a side step. Believe your children if they say they have an invisible friend or that they're hearing Spirit. It's okay to let them run with it. It won't be harmful.

AM: *What advice would you give to children with these abilities?*

James: Acknowledge that you're telling the truth. It doesn't matter if others believe you, you mustn't ever fear their negative judgments. This is the truth. It is your truth, so don't restrain it or suppress it. If at any time you feel fearful, talk to your parents about it. If they don't believe you, find a trusted family member who does because once you can share your truth in a loving circle of support, it will make it much less uncomfortable. Never accept the fearful answers, the "you mustn't," "you shouldn't," or "you can't." Just accept it. It's a gift, your gift. Remember you can always ask Spirit to step back while you need to do something. They'll never impinge or push forward when you don't want them to.

AM: *Thanks so much.*

This section was dedicated to those who are coming next, and will hopefully live in a time when science, mystery and the understanding of Spirit will combine to bring about a new awakening in humanity.

We are all children of a single universe, an act of creation so vast that it is almost beyond imagination. Just as we outgrew the belief the earth was flat, we now need to grow beyond dogmas of the old religions and their divisions, their judgment and hatred of those who are different, the heathen, the infidel, the unworthy, because we are all one. We bleed the same blood and breathe the same air, and most importantly share the same Spirit. It is time we embrace a new concept of Spirit, Creation, Source, and love. We all recognize the power of faith, belief, song and prayer to heal, inspire, and change, but what makes these so powerful? We attribute these transformative powers to something beyond ourselves, but what if it is us who have the ability to transform our lives, and thus the life of all humanity through them? United by a new understanding of Spirit, I believe we can transform our world. The question is what can you do to help bring about this transformation?

Made in the USA
Monee, IL
09 February 2021